The Death Monkey Rides

A Radio Clown's Battle with Thoughts of Suicide

Phil "The Bean" Sisneros

Printed in the United States of America.

For information, please address the author through Jason's Music Publishing, 408 Phoenix Avenue NW, Albuquerque, New Mexico, 87107.

First edition

Library of Congress Cataloguing-in-Publication Data
Sisneros, Phillip The Death Monkey Rides-
A Radio Clown's Battle with Thoughts of Suicide
by Phillip Sisneros ISBN- 978-7351855-4-5
1. Mental Health 2. Memoir 3. Self-help 4. Depression 5. Suicide prevention
10 9 8 7 6 5 4 3 2 1

INTRODUCTION

Beginning in the 1980's, for more than two decades my alter ego, Phil 'The Bean' Sisneros, was a familiar voice in the morning on Albuquerque's KOB-FM radio. I played the mostly funny news guy part of a two-man team, dedicated to waking up our listeners and helping them start their day with a smile. I did my best to amuse and inform folks as they readied themselves for and then made the drive to work as described by Jackson Browne's song, *The Pretender*. The song title accurately mirrored my life at the time. I was not always the joking, fun-loving, everything-is-ok kind of guy, but I pretended to be, at least on the radio.

Not many know what I did for a living before becoming The Bean. Probably fewer knew what I did after I left entertainment radio. I talk about both here. Almost no one knew that I grappled with sometimes severe Depression that often pushed me to that edge that no one likes to think or talk about. This is my message of hope to former listeners and anyone who has dealt with or maybe is still grappling with thoughts of suicide.

AUTHOR'S NOTE

I use a few names for my Depression. I capitalize the word "Depression" because it's that important. I also use Mr. D, the Big-D, the Bastard, the Death Monkey and some other combinations.

The Death Monkey Rides

Prologue

There is an old saying that goes something like this: *Once You're Dead, Life Ain't Worth Livin'*. Despite the silly play on words, the sentiment is not just a joke. For many years I frequently made light of taking my own life and often tried to find humor in suicide.

Sometimes I did this on the radio, hoping to get a laugh out of my audience. Anyone who listened to me knows I always tried to find humor in almost anything, even suicide. I don't do that anymore, and not just because I've been off the air a long time. Killing myself just isn't as funny to me as it once was.

Some time ago an idea started banging around inside my head like a rock in a can. I thought, maybe I should write about my experiences with Depression and how I dealt with it over my years in broadcasting. Maybe because I was once a widely known local radio guy, people might be interested in what the always happy sounding Bean had to say about being sad. And maybe my story could help somebody deal with their own Depression. Maybe writing about it would help *me*. Arguably, because a permanent cure for Depression has yet to be found, maybe we could all learn to keep the sadness genie sleeping in his bottle while we continue to search for a tighter fitting cork. Admittedly, those were a lot of maybes but that is why I decided to share my story.

Long before becoming The Bean on radio, I seldom took anything too seriously, including my physical and mental health. When I finally realized how self-destructive my behaviors had become over the years, it was almost too late. I came close, more than once, to permanently giving up on myself. But luckily, I eventually came to recognize my Depression as the potentially deadly disease that it is and more importantly, to admit to my macho dumb ass that I had to get help from a mental health professional.

I know that a bucket load of celebrities and well-known people have written books about how they dealt with the Big-D. That's wonderful and I strongly encourage more people to talk and/or write about their own struggles. I think we all strive for happiness, whatever that might be for us. Indeed, happiness is subjective and for me, elusive. These words were initially aimed at the relatively few people in the world who may have listened to me on the radio as The Bean or known me in other ways. But if others who never heard of me could benefit, so much the better. Then, like the Covid-19 virus, maybe my story can spread and be passed along to others.

See? I just can't stop trying to make a joke. Seriously though, if just one of you can benefit from these words, that would make me happy. Happiness and Depression don't often mix well, but it can and does happen. If you try, there's no reason you can't squeeze a little Happy out of being Sad. Being happy comes easy for a lot of people, for a long time I wondered why it was so hard for me. I faked it a lot on the radio because I felt it was my job to sound happy. Maybe I just forgot how to be happy for real. Maybe it's about hope after all, even though many of us lose sight of it from time to time.

I've chronicled my life and career, as best as I can recall anyway, before and after The Bean-thing. Through it all, I carried a very Depressed Death Monkey on my back. Most people I mention here are identified by only their first names or initials.

I'm sure other writers have said this, but it really is to protect the innocent…and the guilty. Although, I'm pretty sure the statute of limitations has long since expired for all of us. Again, my life and career journey through Depression serves only as a vehicle to deliver the message that getting therapy can literally be a life saver. So far, it has worked for me. Maybe you will receive the message in my story and as Michelle Obama once advised, "Do something!"

Using my former popularity as a local radio personality as a draw of sorts, I hope to attract interest in learning more about Depression and how it affects people all around you. Lastly, I will likely get some of the details wrong or half-right in my personal story.

Phil Sisneros

Chapter 0 -- What a Long Strange Trip It's Been

~ I sat there in my truck staring through the windshield as I held the Colt .32 in my right hand, a fifth of Jack in my left. In a couple of minutes, I would get out and walk over to a big pine to my left and sit down against the tree, take a last swig then put the gun to my head and pull the trigger.

It was a little after 6 a.m. and still dark as I listened to my partner on the radio, Mike Phillips. He was laughingly telling listeners that The Bean was running a little late and would join him on the air, "any time now…or not. It's hard to tell with this guy, maybe he thought today is Saturday."

A few hours earlier I had driven up to the Jemez Mountains in New Mexico twenty miles from where I grew up and pulled off the road to a spot I knew overlooked the valley and the mountains to the east. I always loved it up here. The sky was starting to lighten up as I told myself how lucky I was to see this one last time.

The Death Monkey Rides

In the early 1980's, it was the sudden death of my friend and radio partner, Steve Hatley, that caused my long simmering Depression to finally boil over and become a suicidal Death Monkey on my back. For so many years before this, my bouts with the Big-D were like rides on the proverbial roller coaster. Up, down. Up, down. But the downs began to go deeper and last longer. The ups began to rise more slowly, did not go as high and didn't last as long.

I thought, mistakenly, that I could fix myself after Steve's death, but I started thinking the only way off the coaster was to jump. Over the years, the thought had briefly crossed my mind, but this may have been the first time I seriously considered suicide, but it would not be the last.

For most of my life before I came to what was called KOB-FM radio at the time, I wrestled with the Depression Bastard, as I began calling it.

Then, for the next two decades on Albuquerque radio and another ten years or so in other jobs, I would win the daily wrestling matches for months at a time and never think about suicide. I laughed more, I had lots of energy, I felt optimistic about the future, life was good all around. But then the Bastard would kick my butt for months as those dark feelings crept back in and I would go back to being sad, angry and hopeless. That was my life for years. During that time I continued to hide the Bastard from everyone while repeatedly promising myself that I would soon surrender myself to a shrink. Of course, I did not seek professional help because I still thought I could learn to beat Depression on my own. Let's pick up this journey at the turning point where I realized that if I did not get help to deal with my Depression, it would likely kill me.

It's been about eight years since I decided retirement would end or at least diminish my Depression. Turns out I was really wrong. Instead, the worst was yet to come. I looked forward to traveling with my wife when I retired. I also dreamed of learning new languages, writing books, connecting with old friends, going to concerts to see my favorite musicians, never wearing a tie again or shaving every day. The last two were about as far as it got. Retirement wasn't as much fun and freedom as I thought it would be.

It is said that time flies when you're having fun. I certainly was not having much fun, and time seemed to drag on, day after day. Those thoughts of cashing in my chips started creeping into my mind again. But this time it was like a brightly lit billboard on I-25 popped up in front of me. It read, *Call A Therapist Today or You Will Die!*

You have probably heard stories about how, after retirement, some men cannot take the lack of purpose and loss of daily personal contact that often comes with retiring. Some men take their own lives as a result. I was headed down that path it seems. Since I must still be alive to write this, you have correctly surmised that I did finally seek professional help. As we navigate the maze ahead, I will explain what happened next and where things stand today.

The Death Monkey Rides

Chapter 1 -- My Depression Begins

Let's roll the tape backward to when I believe my Depression began in earnest, not to be confused with Ernest, who might not appreciate me using his name. As I began writing about the Big-D, I was surprised to find that my troubles likely began at an early age even though I did not know it at the time. For me, it is somewhat comforting to know that this condition did not just appear one day out of nowhere and more importantly, that it was not my fault for developing Depression.

In the early 1940s the federal government took over a small mesa northwest of Santa Fe, New Mexico where the only thing on the site was a prep school for boys. It was easy to defend, militarily and the perfect place for Project Y, a research site that would come to be known as The Manhattan Project. There, the US Government would gather the world's top scientists to develop an atomic bomb.

Los Alamos went from a population of a few young boys and their instructors to almost 6000 scientists and their families almost overnight. After the War, the Lab continued to operate, conducting other top-secret weapons development. By the 1960s, the population was closer to 15,000 people and almost everyone, including my mom and dad, worked for the labs in one capacity or another. That's where I grew up.

In the mid-1950s Santiago Sisneros moved his family to

Los Alamos. Dad, a mid-sized Mexican-American man, 5-foot-seven or so with brown hair and a thin moustache, found work at the Zia company, a U.S. government contractor primarily providing transportation for laboratory personnel. He started out washing vehicles used for government taxis. After 25 years or so, Dad retired after working his way up to middle management in the company. Mom, also Mexican-American, curly hair and about 5'5'' with slightly darker skin than my dad, found work in Los Alamos at the decontamination laundry facility on DP Road. She and others, mostly women, washed and decontaminated clothing worn by scientists and workers who handled radioactive materials used in lab research. She and a number of her fellow workers later developed varying degrees of blotchy skin conditions on their faces and hands, presumably caused by radiation. Luckily, she went on to work at a different job at the Labs, I think she made bomb parts or something. Mom retired from the Labs after a couple of decades.

There were five of us kids. I had two older sisters, Nora and Jennie who lived with my grandparents. Nora was eighteen years older than me and Jennie sixteen years older, and two older brothers, Joe, who was eleven years older than me and Jim or James. I always called him Junior because he was named after my father, Santiago, the equivalent of James in Spanish. Junior was five years my senior.

Joe always seemed to be smiling and took care of me when I was a baby while Mom was at work. He was, and still is, a mostly happy and kind soul. Junior was a nervous-energy type, an always moving kind of guy. He was slightly darker than Joe or me, so we always teased him about it. I think Joe and I even told him he was dark because he was adopted…brothers, right?

Junior was very protective of me. I remember an incident when a neighbor kid, older and bigger than me, was outside in our front yard smacking me around for some reason. Apparently witnessing my beatdown, Junior flew out of our two-story apartment house and chased that kid around the yard until my tormentor collided with the fire escape and crumpled to the ground with a bloody nose and mouth. My brother stood over him and yelled, "You'll get it a lot worse if I ever see you hit my brother again!" We became very close as adults. We fished, hunted, and partied together for many years. We even lived together when we were both divorced and between wives! I loved my brother very much. He died more than a dozen years ago, and I still miss him every day. His death deepened my Depression for a long time. Because I finally sought help, I'm much better now.

And then there was me. Phillip Frederick Cruz Sisneros. From age two to ten, I had a round face, a large forehead and short brown hair. As I grew, I got a little thicker and Mom had to buy "Husky" labeled jeans for me at Clement and Benner, the local department store in Los Alamos. I lost most of that thickness by the time I got to junior high school.

My idea of a good time was plinking rocks onto the roof of a security guard shack. That shack was a checkpoint along the road that ran through Omega Canyon, a highly restricted area connected to the Los Alamos federal government laboratories.

Los Alamos was a small town and there were a lot of people there I didn't know, mostly physicists and other scientists who stayed once the Manhattan Project ended. Some of those folks seemed a bit strange to me. Once when I was twelve, I was walking along Diamond Drive when I came upon a police officer and a motorist he'd pulled over. As I passed, the officer was holding the man's driver's license and asked, "Dr. [whatever his name was], do you realize your license expired in 1952?" The man, who looked a little like Einstein, just shook his head no. I could tell he had much more important things on his mind, like the schematics of a rocket or how to split an atom to be concerned about a damned driver's license. Yeah, the town was full of those types.

I knew a lot of their kids though. Some of them were the ones wearing buttoned-up plaid shirts with pocket protectors holding a slide rule inside. Think Sheldon Cooper from the Big Bang Theory. I think it was a 5th grade classmate of mine whose science project was a huge display that explained the difference between nuclear fission and fusion. The whole class, including the teacher, could only gawk and get out a "Wow!" None of us understood anything about it but it sure looked cool.

Instead of contemplating nuclear physics I spent time amusing myself by flinging stones on top of the aforementioned guard shack until the guard came out and yelled bad things about my momma as he scanned the cliffs above for any sign of his tormentor. Of course, I had squirreled myself away behind a boulder or pine tree and had to stifle my laughter so as not to give away my position. I expected that the guard, who was part of what was called the federal Pro Force guarding the Los Alamos National Laboratory, would call the local town police and they would send an officer or two to drive close to the canyon's edge to look for me. I knew the canyon like the back of my hand, so it was too easy to always elude the long arm of the law. It never occurred to me that they could have apprehended this juvenile delinquent any time they wanted but probably got as much of a kick out of me harassing the laboratory's federal security force as I did.

That's how I spent many summer afternoons when I wasn't pedaling my bike uphill to the nearby reservoir to fish with my buddies. We were always so proud to parade through town with our stringers of trout dangling from the high-rise handlebars of our homemade banana-seat bicycles. I suppose my future problems with authority and abiding love of the outdoors began in those early days. It was about then that something began to happen to me that I didn't understand.

I spent a lot of time with my friends just having fun and being happy but frequently, I just wanted to be by myself and brood over one thing or another. Sometimes I was frustrated because growing up was taking too long. I wanted to learn how to drive a car but was always told I was not old enough yet. I wanted to shoot my dad's big deer rifle, but again, I was too young. Other times I'd sit under a tree staring at the sky, worried that the Russians were going to drop a bomb on me.

At school we had those dumb drills where we pushed our desks against a wall and got under them to protect ourselves from a surprise enemy attack. Maybe it was because of things like that I found myself feeling sad and lonely, maybe even a little frightened. To this day I still don't know why I felt like that sometimes. Luckily, those feelings didn't last very long back then and soon I would put them out of my mind and be OK for a while. I was also good at hiding those strange feelings, I never told anyone. I didn't want anybody to think I was weird, or worse.

In the 1960s, people did not know much about Depression or other mental illnesses. Our impressions were likely based upon movie portrayals of homicidal maniacs and "crazy" people like James Stewart in the film, Harvey. In the movie, Stewart's character claimed to be best friends with a giant rabbit named Harvey, who was invisible to everyone but him. Nut job, right? And who could forget Jack the Ripper? All that people knew was that Jack was a bat-shit-crazy maniac who carved up his victims like he was making a Jack-O-Lantern. Mentally ill people were called lunatics and were forcibly sent to insane asylums. To be clear, I didn't think I was mentally ill and I had never even heard the word Depression. All I knew is that I had these feelings of loneliness and sadness from time to time and something told me I should keep this to myself.

Getting back to my recalcitrant behaviors. It wasn't that I was a bad kid really, more of a prankster, I think. Sometimes I did manage to pull the wool over the eyes of some of my friends' parents who would ask them, "Why can't you be a nice, behaved boy like Phil?" Usually this happened after some mischief we had committed together but I had managed to escape getting caught. Some of my buds called me Eddie Haskell, a reference to the 1960s sitcom Leave It to Beaver about a boy very much like myself who got into all sorts of mischief, but whose understanding parents always were able to forgive and forget.

In the show, Beaver's teenage brother had a friend named Eddie Haskell who was always polite and flattering around adults but the first one to cause trouble. I never missed a chance to display my angel's halo and compliment their moms in order to get on their good side. That was Eddie Haskell's shtick. "That sure is a pretty dress Mrs. Cleaver!" It seemed to work well on the TV show in terms of deflecting blame away from Eddie, who was a devious little shit like me. But I didn't bully anybody. I wasn't a jerk.

I did manage to get into some trouble in the early years. Probably my worst offense was the senseless breaking of windows at a log cabin-like building near the big water tower on 24th St., overlooking Ashley Pond in the middle of town. I was only about ten years old. I still don't remember why I teamed up with a friend to commit such vandalism. I guess we were just bored that night. We were quickly found out by Los Alamos law enforcement and the consequences were swift. My poor dad was summoned to the local police station where I had been taken and informed of my actions. I'm sure Dad was extremely embarrassed by his youngest son's transgression.

Back at home, after being spanked and severely scolded by my dad and mom, I was sent to my room and told I would be imprisoned there for the rest of my life. I was humiliated, ashamed, and extremely sorry for breaking those windows. For weeks, guilt hung over me and I couldn't even look my parents in the eye, especially my dad.

Even though I had a co-conspirator in the crime, I felt like it was all my fault for being so stupid. I brought this mortification to my whole family, and I felt like the worst son, no, the worst person in the world. It was the first time I remember hating myself. I wonder now if that self-loathing, common in Depression, began back then. Even though I did not yet recognize him, the Big-D Bastard had just made a comfortable nest in my head and was planning on a long stay.

Chapter 2 -- Pre-soaking The Bean

I have to start with my parents, right? Alice and Santiago (Jimmy to his non-Spanish speaking bosses and friends.) Mom was adamant about teaching me to be self-sufficient. I learned how to cook, clean house, wash and iron my own clothes, etc. "Don't expect some woman to do these things for you," she'd say. Funny how I slowly forgot how to do some of that stuff after leaving bachelorhood behind. Yeah, I just got lazy. But I will always be thankful to her for helping me to be self-sufficient. I also admired her for never taking crap from anyone, man or woman, but especially men. I think she was a feminist before being that was a thing.

However, along with being extremely independent, Mom possessed almost no social filters. She always spoke her mind, even at the expense of decorum and often with little regard for hurting people's feelings. *Blunt* is a good word to describe my mother's frequent behavior, defined as '*...the fact of being very direct and of saying exactly what you think without trying to be polite.'* The operative word there is 'polite.' When called out about her inappropriate stinging comments, she simply replied, "Well, it's the truth!"

Sometimes her words made me sad when they were directed at me. I often asked myself, 'Does she dislike me or was it something I said or did to deserve it?' When she directed her rude comments to others, if I was present, I felt like crawling under a rock from embarrassment. Clearly, her words were often hurtful, but I guess I just adapted what my siblings and others said, "Well, that's just the way she is."

A classic example of Mom's insensitivity occurred one day when I was in high school and a friend, whom I had known for years, came to the house to pick me up for some activity or event. The girl, who many years later became a sister-in-law to me, was clearly a little shocked when Mom turned from the front door and yelled upstairs to me, "Phillip, your fat friend is here!"

I was mortified when I heard what she said. Although my friend had a good sense of humor and just laughed it off, I had to believe her feelings were hurt. But to this day, when my forgiving sister-in-law and I recall the incident, we both get an ironic chuckle out of Mom's relentless bluntness.

Another example makes me laugh out loud when I recall the night dear ol' Mom got so mad at me and my brothers that she stormed out of the house and vowed never to return. Joe was about seventeen years old; Junior was about eleven and I was around six. Dad must have been working late because it was just us boys and her. I don't remember what we did, but it really pissed her off. As she grabbed her purse and car keys she yelled, "I'm sick and tired of you little sons-a-bitches! I'm leaving!"

She stormed out the front door, jumped in the car and drove off. We ran to the window and watched her burn rubber down the street. Of course, we could not believe she just left us, and we were scared to death of what our Pops would do when he found out. We didn't know if he would be mad at her or us. But more than that, my angry mother just said she was sick and tired of me. I was devastated. I was too young to understand adult temper tantrums, so I just cried.

We were still staring out the window in disbelief when she flew by the house in the car on the street. A couple of minutes later she drove by again, this time a little more slowly. We lost track of how many times Mom drove around the block. She finally parked out front and began lighting cigarettes, one after another, for about a half hour. When she finally began to get out of the car, Joe pulled Junior and me away from the window and said, "OK, you guys go to your room and close the door and don't say a word."

For years we hardly spoke about the incident. If Dad knew he never mentioned it and neither did Mom. As adults though, we sometimes recounted 'The Night Mom Ran Away from Home' and teased her about it while laughing our butts off. I guess we got over the hurt and fear. As we told the story she would give us the death stare that all moms have but then she would start laughing with us.

Did her bluntness and impulsive actions affect my Depression? It made me angry and hurt and sometimes, I felt no love or sympathy for her because of her meanness. Then I would feel guilty for not loving my own mother. Anger, guilt, confusion, and sadness; I was young and did not know how to deal with these mixed emotions. Hell, I don't think I even knew my feelings were called emotions.

Sometimes, after a run-in with Mom, I would wander off to the edge of one of the nearby canyons and marvel at the scenery, fling pinecones over the cliff and daydream. I envisioned myself as an explorer, traveling through the Alaskan wilderness with a team of sled dogs, living off the land and discovering the ruins of an ancient civilization encased in snow and ice. I would become world famous for finding evidence of people who lived thousands of years before mankind was believed to have originated. Sometimes I would imagine life as something other than a human, like a dog, a bird, even a tree. I would ask myself out loud, "What would that be like?"

I even made-up scenarios where I was Superman and I married Lois Lane and we flew to other worlds and had kids who had superpowers! (More on such thoughts later.) Pretty soon I would forget about being in trouble with Mom. I thought maybe I was just too sensitive and got my feelings hurt too easily. Other times, I just wanted to sit quietly under a tree and not think about anything. The idea of being in broadcasting would be born decades later.

Distancing myself from hurtful feelings wasn't always easy, sometimes it was sort of like filling my pants pockets with rocks and trying to swim across the Rio Grande during the Spring run-off when the current was swiftest, unable to keep from drowning. So yes, her sharp-tongued bull-in-the-china-shop commentaries definitely added to my Depression, even though I did not yet know what that meant.

Fortunately, I was not alone in bearing the brunt of the Wrath of Mom. My older brothers and sisters had their share of deep criticisms and bluntness from our mother. Surely, they experienced some lasting effects from that, but I do not know how they dealt with it. My sisters Nora and Jennie were on their own before I was growing up in Los Alamos. And Joe and Junior were out of the nest by the time I got to junior high, so it was just me at home until I graduated high school.

Over the years ahead into my adulthood, Mother continued to consistently criticize my life choices such as girlfriends, my physical appearance, the fact that I didn't speak Spanish well, etc. For example, she referred to one college girlfriend as 'moon faced, too skinny, and a 'gringa.' (White girl.) I was always 'too fat' in her eyes, and she seldom missed a chance to remind me. Mostly I ignored it all, or so I thought. In retrospect, I did not completely ignore the criticisms and mean comments. Instead, I simply allowed them to pile up and weigh me down like a backpack full of sand and rocks. (My pants pockets were too small by then.) That pack was just something I carried around on my back all the time, like the proverbial monkey, it became something I got used to. I had no idea how heavy that monkey would become.

It would be unfair of me to blame all my Depression problems on my mother. Of course, her caustic criticisms and other comments certainly did not help matters, but she was not a monster. I have to believe she loved me and my brothers and sisters. She showed her love in all the usual ways that most mothers do, and I believe she was never purposely cruel to me or my siblings. I think she just did not realize how hurtful her words could be, especially to her own children. I also believe she learned her bad behavior from her own mother who, by all accounts, was especially mean to her. Mom was an only child, so she had no one else to share the pain inflicted by an abusive parent. A mental health professional could surely explain that better than I can.

Next up among the people who helped shape me is Dad. During my early years my Pops did his best to teach me the responsibilities of becoming a man and a good person in general. He would frequently tell me, "Treat people like you want to be treated, but don't ever let anybody run you over, either." He also reminded me that I was born a poor Mexican and would likely die a poor Mexican. In retrospect, that seems a little fatalistic, no? Optimism was not my father's forte. But his guidance served me well and I tried to emulate him and be the good guy that he always was to me.

I do not attribute to him any of the hurtful meanness and bully-like behavior that I experienced from my mother. Contrastingly, as I got older, Dad seemed to sense when I was depressed and he would offer to listen to whatever was bothering me and then try to offer some words of encouragement. Unlike Mom, Dad was always fairly quiet, not often prone to explosive anger or harsh words to us kids. I do remember him yelling at my mother a couple of times, over what I don't know, but overall, he was a mellow kind of guy.

He was, however, strict when it came to disciplining me for bad behavior and didn't hesitate to bring out the belt when I deserved it. Lucky for me, I didn't always get caught.

Among other people who had a profound effect on my life is my high school football coach, Glenn Howell. I can still hear him telling us that there would be times during a game, late in the fourth quarter, when we were exhausted and maybe behind by a touchdown or two, and we felt like we were going to lose. He'd say, "That's when you just suck it up, forget the pain, forget how tired you are and find the strength you didn't even know you had, leave it all out there on the field!"

Of course, we did not win every game but because of his words, I knew I had done my best. The message: *Don't give up, no matter how bad things may be, don't give up.*

Later in my life, on numerous occasions when I was down and almost out for one reason or another, I'd hear Coach Howell in my mind yelling, "C'mon Sis! (short for Sisneros) it's the fourth quarter, suck it up!" Most times his words worked and helped me to crawl out from under my Depression boulder. Sometimes the words did not help, and for a while I would wallow in self-pity and self-destructive behavior. More importantly though, on many occasions I found the mental and physical strength to move through my Depression thanks to Coach Howell's football field exhortations. I still hear and use his words.

Chapter 2 -- My Edukashun

Once again, to use outdated radio terminology, let's roll back the tape. Recording tape isn't used anymore, everything is digitized these days.

Turns out, my education at Los Alamos High School was pretty boring for me so I could never really get serious about anything other than football and girls. Not that I was too smart for the room, my grades were about average, but none of the classroom subjects produced that aha moment where I suddenly said to myself, "This is what I wanna do for the rest of my life."

But it wasn't all boring. In my junior year at Los Alamos High School, I met and fell in love with SM who was one year ahead of me. With her help, I managed to not flunk algebra, mostly because she did my homework for me. Imagine my parents' surprise when they learned that SM and I were engaged to be married. Apparently, she had told her parents about our plans, and they immediately took out an engagement announcement in the local newspaper.

Somehow, I had forgotten to mention our sometime-in-the-future nuptials to my folks. Hell, I wasn't even eighteen years old yet! The day of the newspaper announcement my mother came home from work with her hair on fire. She shook the engagement announcement in my face and loudly recounted how her fellow workers were congratulating her on her son's plans to marry. Apparently, she smiled a lot and thanked them for their congratulations even though it was the first she had heard of those plans.

Then my dad got home from work. He had not yet cleared the front door when my mother held up the newspaper announcement in front of him. He was obviously confused and annoyed, but he took the paper and sat down at the kitchen table to read what Mom had shoved in his face. After what seemed like forever, Dad put down the announcement and looked over his reading glasses at me and simply said, "Like hell you are." SM and I never made it to the altar.

It was not long after that debacle that I developed a special interest in my senior English class, or I should say, my English teacher. She was in her early twenties and smokin' hot! I just knew I could make her leave her husband and run off with one of her soon to be eighteen-year-old students; me. But it was merely another one of my myriad fantasies that continues to plague my life to this day.

For example, while still in high school, instead of listening to the math teacher who was explaining Pascal's Triangle one day, I was gathering wool in my head and imagining that I discovered the cure for cancer. Then, as the fantasy progressed, my discovery led to teaming up with a quantum physics scientist, who just happened to be an impossibly beautiful woman. Together, we then developed some sort of gadget that enabled interstellar travel to distant galaxies. I never did learn what that triangle thing was. Later in my life, one former girlfriend or wife, I forget which, told me that in my head I lived in Disneyland, specifically Fantasyland. I guess she wasn't wrong, right?

After graduation from Los Alamos High School, I

attended a computer programming school in Kansas City, Missouri. I think I went because a buddy of mine was also going and we both thought we could be president of IBM someday. But mostly I think Marty and I were just excited to be away from home in a big city for the first time in our young lives.

We lived in a huge boarding house with about 30 other guys from all over the country. We had an incredibly good time while forging a lifetime of memories and, oh yeah, we learned a little bit about computer programming. In 1970, computer programming for industry was a complicated process. It consisted of writing directions for a computer key punch machine, an electromechanical device that allowed users to manually "punch" holes in stiff cards allowing operators to translate lines of code or data into specific patterns. These little paper cards would then be fed into a large mainframe computer which would then spit out reams of paper that somebody would ostensibly use to make a payroll plan for some business or something equally boring.

After graduation and spending a great deal of our parents' money on schooling, neither Marty nor I would go on to have a career in computers. But I did fall in love with a cute girl from Arkansas who was in Kansas City to attend stewardess school. In the 70's, flight attendants were called stewardesses. I wanted to marry her, but she was smart enough to go on to have a long career as a flight attendant instead. Of course I was crushed, but in those days, I was still able to handle a break-up without too much damage to my male ego. Depression had not yet germinated into the fields of hemlock it would later become.

With ~~a~~ computer programming degree in hand, I returned to New Mexico and enrolled at the University of New

Mexico in Albuquerque in hopes of learning something else I could do for a living. After some uncertainty about what I really wanted to study, for some reason I chose to major in English. The curriculum included a class in Writing and Communication which, at the time, was offered by the Journalism Department. I liked the class so much I decided to switch majors to Journalism with Spanish as a minor.

My Spanish still sucks but my major was how I started training to become a journalist. In the beginning I could not decide if I wanted to be a print journalist or try newswriting for radio or television. Of course, I chose broadcasting because, as the saying goes, I had a great face for radio. But TV was more glamorous and being in front of a camera like my idols, CBS news anchor Walter Cronkite and the NBC news team of Chet Huntley and David Brinkley were where I wanted to be. So, TV news, here I come!

Around that same time, I had my first mental flameout due to Depression. I do not remember what triggered the episode, but I quit going to classes and retreated to my apartment for several days. For some reason, or perhaps no reason at all, sadness and thoughts of dropping out of school had suddenly fallen over me. I was so down that I called my folks at one in the morning on a weeknight and when my dad asked what was wrong, all I could do was sob and say I really didn't know. Less than two hours later my father knocked on my apartment door. He had driven from Los Alamos to Albuquerque in record time in the middle of the night. We just talked about nothing in particular until dawn. Of course, he asked me what had happened to send me into a tailspin and when I said I was not sure, he let it go at that. I guess just having Dad there listening to me made all the difference.

Finally, I felt better and told my father he was going to

be late for work so he should get back home. He wouldn't leave until I could assure him that whatever had happened was over and I was OK. I did so and he left for home and another full day of work without any sleep this time. Apparently, I had indeed sucked it up and managed to move forward that day. Thanks to my Pops and the words of my high school football coach I got through it.

Looking back, as opposed to high school, college was so much more engaging for me in terms of classes that could be tailored to actually help shape my future. I wasn't really sure where broadcasting would take me, but I reasoned that news writing and reporting could not only be creative, but it would also be fun to focus on telling true stories about everyday events. I looked forward to almost every class I chose, particularly those that touched on law and ethics in journalism. Later, I would learn just how important facts and legal responsibilities are in news gathering, writing and reporting.

Chapter 3 -- First Job in Broadcasting

In the second half of my junior year at UNM, I took a practicum class that placed me at KGGM-TV, channel 13 in Albuquerque. It was the mid-70's. The station later changed call letters to the current KRQE.

Essentially, it was an unpaid internship to get experience in various facets of television news. I learned how to research and write news stories, use film cameras, edit film and be in front of a camera. To my surprise, when the class ended, I was offered a job at the station. I immediately withdrew from college, figuring I just landed the job I had hoped I'd get with a journalism degree so why wait? The opportunity might never come again. And so began my career in broadcasting as a TV news reporter/photographer and eventually a fill-in anchorman of the weekend newscast. I was in broadcasting Heaven.

Walter Cronkite was in no danger of me ever taking his anchor job on the CBS Evening News, but I was determined to make my mark in Albuquerque television news. My very first story was, in my mind, an Emmy Award-winning investigative piece entitled *Cow Ravages Local Dump.* I was sent to the municipal landfill located on Nine Mile Hill just a bit west of Albuquerque to chronicle the sudden appearance of an escaped cow from nearby ranchland. That's the kind of story that made the news in 1975.

After watching my story that night, my brother Jim handed me a beer and said, "Here's to my brother, the fearless hot shot TV reporter who chases vicious cows around the dump!" I had to start somewhere, right? I cannot remember being depressed at that time. The excitement of my first job and the sense that it could lead to a career doing something that really mattered to me must have eclipsed the Big-D, at least for the near future.

Later that year I was sent north to Holman, New Mexico to cover the sudden appearance of an apparition of Jesus Christ on a local church building wall. Hundreds had begun traveling to the tiny village to witness what many were calling a miracle; others were claiming the apparition signaled the end of the world. Of course, I interviewed several of the faithful for their take on what they had seen. Personally, I could only make out something resembling a face on the wall, but it also looked like a water stain.

Anyway, we did our best to capture the image on film but, as I soon learned back at the station, nothing but an old, weathered adobe wall appeared on the footage. However, since we were a CBS network affiliate, I called the New York Desk and hurriedly recounted the story and asked if they wanted me to send it to them for use on the Evening News. The unenthusiastic editor asked, "Does the story include an interview with the Jesus guy? If not, we're gonna have to pass." Once again, Walter Cronkite had nothing to fear from me.

Then I was assigned to cover a session of the state legislature in Santa Fe. Lots of juicy political stories for a nascent reporter. At the time, reporters often had to be their own photographers too. So besides having to drive back and forth each day from Albuquerque to the Capitol, I had to carry around an ancient film camera the size of a Volkswagen and its wood and metal tripod, which together, had to weigh at least fifty pounds. But I also got to learn a lot about how the sausage is made in state government and how the democratic process works or doesn't. I knew I had been given a chance to prove myself as a reporter and I was determined to make the most of it. I became laser focused on honing my newfound craft.

Around the same time, I somehow talked a fantastic woman into marrying me. Looking back, despite good intentions, I soon learned that I was not ready to settle down. Somehow, even though I had a great new wife and my new dream job, I wasn't happy or satisfied with my good fortunes. I felt anxious all the time, and I was constantly and secretly feeling down in the dumps and I did not know why.

Unfortunately, the stress of making a good impression at work and learning how to be married suddenly produced feelings of self-doubt and self-destructive behaviors like drinking, smoking pot, and cheating on my new wife. Yes, like a huge dumbass and world class jerk, I cheated on her. I was in my early twenties and too stupid to know what I had but I soon found out what I lost. I was the pilot of that plane and for no reason, I flew it straight into the ground. No excuses, I alone blew up the marriage and caused hurt and confusion to a wonderful lady who loved me. Chalk up divorce number one. I consider that failure to be one of the biggest regrets of my life.

Even though I had known since childhood that occasionally I could be a little gloomy and feel isolated, it was easy to snap out of it and get back to whatever was normal for a kid. But now, as a young adult, it seemed like someone or something was often controlling my life and all I could do was watch it happen.

For the first time, I started to worry about my behavior and feelings of sadness and being alone. Was this just temporary like when I was a child or was I beginning to go a little bonkers? Say hello to my little friend and puppet master. The Depression Bastard was knocking on my door.

Phil Sisneros

Chapter 4 -- Marriage Crashes as Career Takes Off

Drugs and alcohol had become my constant companions during my first marriage. I felt worthless, guilty and angry at myself all the time now. I thought the booze and drugs were helping me deal. They were not. I could not explain my actions to myself or anyone who may have asked, "What the hell are you doing?" It was as though something was chasing me and I had to run. So, I did. Much later, my own research found that this is called Psychological Avoidance or 'the conscious or unconscious efforts to avoid dealing with a stressor to protect oneself from discomfort or negative emotions.'

Then completely out of nowhere, I received a call from a former technical director at KGGM who was now working at a TV station in Phoenix. He said they were looking for a reporter to replace another who was leaving and that I should immediately send them my air check, or videotape resume. Next thing I knew, I was the new guy at KPHO-TV, Channel 5. I kiddingly became known as "Carlos' Replacement," the reporter I was supposed to replace but who never left after all.

Apparently, they needed another reporter anyway. I was hired and once again, I was in broadcasting Heaven. It didn't sink in until later that I had just left behind a loving wife, friends and family and everything that was my life in New Mexico. I didn't know it yet, but all those dark feelings I was running from apparently hitched a ride to join me in Arizona.

My elation over my new and better job was only slightly diminished when my first assignment was an uncontrolled fire at…wait for it…a metal junk yard! OK, it wasn't a dump exactly and there wasn't a cow in sight. However, it felt like a thousand degrees outside, and I was instantly drenched in sweat. Apparently, a pile of pipes that contained magnesium somehow caught fire, and it was melting all the other stacks of piping nearby. It was a big deal because there were structures adjacent to the yard that were in danger of burning.

My photographer rightly predicted that the story would only merit 30 seconds of tape and a voiceover report by one of the anchor people, using facts that I would provide. To his credit, he did tell me I should just stay in the air-conditioned news vehicle while he took the necessary video. But, being the new guy in town, I thought I should be out there doing my reporter stuff no matter what the conditions were at the scene. As a result, I almost suffered heat stroke and had to dry clean my sport jacket, tie and pants which had all been soaked in sweat. Welcome to Phoenix in June.

Luckily, the news stories I covered quickly got better and more consequential. Since I had some experience, I was frequently assigned to cover state and local government happenings. Pretty dry stuff most of the time but interesting too. And it was good experience for a political job I would take years later.

Perhaps the biggest story I covered in Phoenix was one of the most infamous murders in Arizona history. It was the 1976 car bombing of Arizona Republic investigative reporter Don Bolles. The mob-style murder was surrounded in intrigue with suspected involvement by organized crime, real estate moguls, politicians and others. It was a case so complicated and wide ranging that every reporter on staff at KPHO-TV covered a piece of the story at one time or another. Eventually, the informant Bolles was supposed to meet with, and his handlers were convicted and sent to prison. It was the first time I realized how dangerous journalism could be. Nonetheless, I felt lucky to be a part of the national free press although sometimes journalists paid the ultimate price for that freedom.

Another story that made national headlines was one of the crazier ones that I reported on. It involved the 1977 hijacking and robbery of an armored car and the grisly murders of the two guards. Authorities followed leads that took them from northern Arizona to Lake Mead in Nevada. In the beginning there was some speculation that maybe the guards had simply stolen more than $200,000 and vanished. Eventually, authorities indicated that the guards were innocent and had likely been killed and their bodies hidden.

Our own investigation led us to the Navajo Nation in northeastern Arizona where we learned that an old woman there, known as a psychic of sorts, might be able to help provide information on the crime. We gave her all the facts we had about the hijacking and robbery and a small amount of cash. The woman then allowed my photographer Dan and I to witness, but not record, a ceremony in her small home in which she sprinkled corn dust and recited incantations while waving her hands over us. The whole thing was spooky.

When she finished the ceremony, the old woman told us her visions indicated that the two armored car guards were dead. She also said she saw a huge lake and that the men's corpses were beneath the surface. We left immediately and headed for Lake Mead on the Arizona/Nevada border which was the closest large body of water.

We chartered a boat the next morning and spent the day searching areas that the old woman had described as possible sites where the bodies were located. Of course we found nothing. Our boss told us to return to Phoenix forthwith. Since the only footage we had was of our boat ride and general area, our news director decided we didn't have enough to make a credible story. After spending four days and a ton of the station's money we came back with zilch. We did inform law enforcement about our efforts and the psychic's conclusions. We were politely thanked and that was the end of it for us.

Turns out the old lady psychic was right. Weeks later the armored car drivers' bodies were recovered in Lake Mead. After almost a year, two brothers, Michael and Patrick Poland were charged with murder and robbery and executed by the State of Arizona. It was the biggest story I never got to tell.

The big news stories notwithstanding, during my time at KPHO, three of my colleagues and I managed to engage in all manner of after-work debauchery and excess. I and the aforementioned Dan, Carlos, whom I did not replace, and Jack became the Four Musketeers of partying and living La Vida Loca.

We could always be found at the Stag and Hound restaurant and bar, conveniently located across the parking lot from our studios. It was an air-conditioned place to cool off after work, a place where I could wear my Happy-Go-Lucky mask and nobody was the wiser. Being depressed was not something I was ready to fully admit to myself, much less have others suspect about me. Therefore, I presented the persona of the fun-loving, hard-partying, menudo-loving new guy from Albuquerque.

As the months passed and my brain evaporated due to

the relentless heat, despite the good times, I frequently found myself in my apartment alone, except for a bottle of whiskey to help dull my feelings of regret and self-loathing. I hated myself for leaving my first wife for no good reason and causing her the mental anguish she must have felt. I hated the heat in Phoenix. I hated that I had just wrecked a brand-new car because I was drunk. I hated that I was so lonely now and that it all was my own doing.

It had taken years, but I finally allowed myself to admit that I might be depressed, although in the mid 1970's I think it was still being referred to as *melancholia* by professionals and more commonly described as *the blues*, *down in the dumps,* or being *bummed out*. Whatever it was called I knew it was not normal and that I had it. That is when I started trying to learn more about what was wrong with me. At the time, such mental problems were just not talked about and there definitely was a palpable stigma attached to such emotions. Consequently, there was not much I was able to learn about what we now know as clinical Depression. Fortunately, today much more is known and written about symptoms, triggers, effects, who could suffer from it, and how to manage it, etc.

I was still keeping that part of my life under wraps because of the potential stigma, in my mind anyway, of being perceived as something other than a fun loving, hard-charging TV news guy. I never talked about Depression with anyone, especially friends and coworkers. Can you imagine blurting out, "Hey, I'm really depressed and I feel like I'm drowning here." My compadres likely would have told me to drown my sorrows in another beer and snort up a line of cocaine. I was still unconvinced that I needed someone to explain and help me deal with all these dark thoughts. Somehow, I survived Phoenix, despite myself.

Chapter 5 -- Welcome to Hollywood

My next job as a TV reporter was at KHJ-TV, Channel 9 in Los Angeles, later to become KCAL-TV. I was hired away from Phoenix to become a general assignment reporter. Both of my sisters and one of my brothers lived in the Los Angeles area so I would be near family. I had finally made it to the big time in my mind. Additionally, I could not get over the fact that I had a cameraman *and* a soundman to accompany me to each story. My life could not get any better.

One of my first assignments involved a guy who sat down in the intersection of Hollywood Boulevard and Vine Street and proceeded to pour gasoline over himself and light a match. Of course, I jumped out of our news unit and began to prepare to do a 'stand up' as it's called in TV news parlance. But my crew politely told me it would not be necessary, they would get a little bit of footage and sound and then let the editors and writers back at the studios do their thing. I started to protest and the sound guy quickly spoke up, "Phil, new-to-L.A. reporters usually start out as pretty much just glorified microphone holders so don't take it personally, once you get the lay of the land, *then* we throw you to the wolves!" Welcome to Hollywood.

I'll admit my ego was a little bruised at first, but I quickly got over it. TV news in Los Angeles was a whole different animal than anything I had ever experienced. The first thing I had to do was become a member of two unions, the American Federation of Radio and Television Artists (AFTRA) and the Screen Actors Guild (SAG). No one had mentioned that detail before I came to L.A. but, when in Rome, right? Also, up until now, instead of just myself and a film/videotape editor being mostly the only ones responsible for getting a story on the air, at KHJ, there was a phalanx of newsroom warriors who had a piece of any field reporter's story.

Accompanying me on everyday stories there was a camera operator and a sound person and sometimes a field producer if it was a multifaceted and complicated story…think presidential visit. Back at the studio, the assignments editor, who also functioned as a script copy editor, reviewed my initial writing. Then, a news writer finessed the script and worked with a film and videotape editor to put it all together.

Finally, a producer would review the package, including my on-camera intro and close and make any necessary changes if needed. Only then would my story be entered into the queue for that night's newscast. There were a few times when the story I had originally envisioned did not exactly match what ultimately made the air. I learned that a good reporter sometimes had to check his/her ego at the door and work with other professionals whose job it was to make sure the finished product was the best it could be.

Nonetheless, the excitement of working in TV news in Los Angeles was almost overwhelming. It truly was fireworks, unicorns and confetti. All was right with the world. Unfortunately, Mr. D was still with me, always lurking in the shadows, like an emotional vampire waiting to suck out my excitement. Sometimes, I was powerless to even acknowledge

The Bastard to myself, but I knew he was there. Have you ever had the dream where you see the monster across the bedroom, but you are paralyzed and can't even scream? It was like that. But the Depression was tamped down at the moment. Working as a reporter in the second largest television news market in the country was providing enough distraction for the time being.

Another big, but very welcome, distraction was living in Redondo Beach. I had the perfect bachelor pad, an ocean view apartment in a large complex that was only yards from the waves and the famous Redondo Beach Pier. The place had restaurants, a fish market, and nightclubs all around. Everything a wild and crazy guy like me could ever hope for.

A couple of my old buddies from Phoenix had scored great jobs at a San Diego TV station and it was only a two-hour drive away, so the party boys were back together and still livin' La Vida Loca. I was happy, I was relaxed, I was satisfied with my life, and did I mention I was happy?

Chapter 6 -- Oops, I Do it Again!

Then something completely unexpected happened, I fell in love again!

It had not even been a year in L.A. when I got married for the second time. It was fitting that I met her, let's just call her KR, while on a news story assignment. My soundman noticed the mutual initial attraction between us and badgered me into asking her out. Of course, one thing led to another and yada, yada, it wasn't long before we eloped to Long Beach, a few miles down the coast and got married on the permanently docked Queen Mary. It turns out that boats and marriage don't always mix well, as you will see.

Neither of us invited family members to the ceremony. Her parents in northern California, who apparently were well off, did not approve of me. They told her I did not make enough money to support her in the style to which she was accustomed. To be fair, she had previously married a member of a famously rich family and spent a six-month honeymoon sailing the world on his giant custom catamaran. They divorced soon after their return. I'm guessing that after half a year at sea the romance sort of foundered, proving once again that money cannot always buy happiness, although it can keep it afloat for a while anyway.

My family was aware that we were getting married but

not when, since we had not set a date. Most of my side thought my dearest was a bit snooty and difficult to warm up to. My oldest sister was apoplectic when she learned that my love intended to keep her maiden name for professional reasons, and because she was an only child, she wanted to keep her family name as long as possible. That was OK with me. Given the feelings harbored by both our families we decided our union would only be witnessed by four of our friends.

Despite my increasingly frequent brooding and despondent feelings, the first year was great. I left behind my beach-bachelor pad, and we moved into a comfortable apartment in Glendale, not far from downtown Los Angeles. We had a party in our new place and invited a few of KR's friends and my old TV news colleagues from San Diego and Phoenix. My Vida Loca buds and I drank, smoked Mexican Laughing Tobacco, and did lines of cocaine; our usual party behavior over the past few years. At one point I realized KR's friends had left the party, and she was sitting in a corner watching us with curiosity and obvious annoyance. "Uh-oh," I thought to myself. But I quickly dismissed the thought and went out on our balcony for some air and to smoke another joint with one of the guys.

One of my Musketeers had already fallen off a high stool at our small bar and then passed out on the couch. Dan-D had gone over to talk with KR when he noticed she was giving all of us the stink eye. He talked with KR for a little while then came out on the balcony where Jack-G and I were 'getting smart,' as I called it. Dan-D leaned over as I passed him the joint and in a low voice said, "Your lady does not like us. She told me we were drug addicts and drunks. For fifty bucks I'll toss her off the balcony if you want." The three of us roared with laughter. Dan-D was joking of course but I got the message. Oops, I thought, I did it again. This was years before the Britney Spears song.

Things blew over after a while. Then KR and I decided to purchase a small house in Tujunga, a little further north of Glendale. It wasn't in the greatest neighborhood, but it was what we could comfortably afford. The commute to our respective jobs was a few minutes longer but, in Los Angeles, distance is measured by how long it takes to get there, not how far it is from where you are.

We became a typical suburban couple complete with two dogs and a mortgage. One of those pups was Garbanzo, as in the bean, a very large blond Irish Wolfhound mix, rescued from the Burbank animal shelter. He would later come back to New Mexico with me and his name was a contributing factor in why I was comfortable calling myself The Bean on 93.3 KOB-FM radio. I frequently took Garbanzo fishing and hiking with me, so we became close buddies, he was my best friend in fact. Our other dog, a Beagle, was acquired sometime later and I named him Munchie. Yeah, I know, there was probably some psychological significance as to why I gave them those specific names, but I forgot. Something about short term memory loss I heard.

One fateful weekend I took the dogs to the nearby San Gabriel Mountains. My wife had some work-related event to attend so she could not accompany us. That made me angry and sad because I considered the short trip a family outing where KR could experience the outdoors and thus share my love of the mountains. She grew up a city girl whose idea of the outdoors was a city park. I got really pissed and hurt that she had other plans.

I later learned my negative reaction was likely caused by my Depression. When I got up into the mountains, instead of fishing or hiking with my dogs, I just found a picnic ground, parked, sat in the front seat and began drowning my sorrows with a case of beer and a bottle of whiskey. Of course, Garbanzo and Munchie got restless in the back of my camper-shell-covered pickup truck, so I let them out do their business and then sat on the tailgate until they came back. They were thirsty so I filled their water bowls while I drank beer and sipped whiskey. As I began to feel the effects of the booze, I offered them some beer which they lapped up. Pretty soon it was one beer for me and one for them to share. I did not offer my Jack Daniels though, that seemed over the line.

I soon drifted off to sleep. When I woke up, the dogs were snoring and there were empty beer cans scattered around the truck bed but I somehow managed to hold on to the bottle of hooch. I surmised that all three of us had taken a nap in the truck. It was starting to get dark, so I closed up the camper with the still sleeping dogs inside and headed for home.

When I pulled into my driveway, I saw that the wife was home, she came outside when she saw us arrive. I got out and went around to the back of my truck to let the boys out. They were both still sprawled out and there was dog vomit all over the place. I felt the presence of a very pissed off wife standing next to me, she was just staring at the dogs, the mess, and me. She turned, stormed into the house and slammed the front door behind her. Looking at my sad-eyed, sick looking pups, I said out loud, “Shit boys, we in trouble now.” In retrospect, I think that incident was another nail in the coffin of my second marriage.

Luckily, my stupid and cruel behavior with the dogs was eventually forgiven after a heartfelt and sincere apology and a promise that it would never happen again. I was beginning to think I had a real drinking problem…duh! But I quickly recalled a drinking buddy's creed, *I drink, I get drunk, I fall down, no problem!* Yeah, I was headed for trouble.

Meanwhile, I had always wanted to buy some mountain land and live out my days hunting, fishing, hiking, and all the other things you do in my version of Heaven. We started looking around New Mexico first. We could not find any tracts of mountain land we could afford so we went north, looking for that Rocky Mountain high in Colorado. We found it near Fairplay, seventy acres of aspens, pines and open space. We planned to build a home and retire there when the time came.

Around the same time, wife Numero Dos's career with the Los Angeles City Schools skyrocketed. She was promoted to be the head of the district's Bilingual Education department. And I was beginning to build a name for myself as a reporter, or perhaps that was wishful thinking. Anyway, I should have been on Cloud Nine, right? But Depression does not make sense most of the time. Here I was working the best job of my career so far, I had married a gorgeous and brilliant lady, and yet soon found myself ambling into a certain bar almost every day after work. I believed a couple of drinks could help me shake growing feelings of doubt, hopelessness and sorrow. But what the hell did I have to doubt, to be hopeless about, to be sad about? Nothing I could pinpoint. Depression does not need a reason.

The hugely famous Nickodell Restaurant and Bar was located between Channel 9 and Paramount Studios on Melrose Avenue in Hollywood. Literally steps away from the TV station's front door, the bar became a convenient place for me to wind down from a day of covering the news in and around Los Angeles. It was the type of bar where the bartenders covered for guys whose wives were always calling, looking for their husbands. It also quickly became the place for me to try to drown that damned Depression which had come racing back into my life with lights and sirens. Soon I became distant, listless and increasingly unhappy with my homelife life in general. I did not realize it yet, but my second wife and I were beginning to really grow apart. All my fuckups were adding up and I could see it in her face.

Then an incredible opportunity presented itself and my Depression abated somewhat. I suddenly had a chance to tour Europe. My brother and his partner were soon leaving and asked if I was interested in going with them. Of course, I said yes. Only there was a big problem, I hadn't been at KHJ long enough yet to accrue much vacation time. I figured I would just ask my boss if I could take three weeks off without pay. It was an extreme longshot but I had to ask, right?

My news director just stared at me for what seemed like forever.

Finally, she asked, "Have you ever been to Europe before?" I replied that I had not, and expected her to say, "Well, that's going to have to wait if you want to continue working here." But after a long pause, she smiled and told me that she was about my age, mid-twenties, when she had an opportunity to go to Europe and her boss allowed her the time off to go. "I have never forgotten that experience and how it helped me appreciate what we have here in our country and how people in other countries live," she said. "Make your plans, I'll set it up with management." I could only stare back at her, slack-jawed and stunned for a few seconds. In my head, "She just said I could go!" I thanked her profusely and walked out of her office in a daze.

The trip to Europe was monumental in more ways than the obvious. On the very long flight from New York to Shannon, Ireland, I inexplicably and instantly fell in love with

Colleen, her real name. In this case I'll use her real name because it is <u>*so*</u> Irish and I know she will never see this book. She was a strikingly attractive flight attendant from County Cork, Ireland. Anyway, I think she loved me too, fleetingly at least. At the rear of the plane, between her having to take care of passengers, we talked for hours during the flight. Upon landing, on the way out of the plane, we embraced and kissed hello and goodbye. We were both married but agreed that in a different time and place, we could have been together. I did not doubt that for a moment. I didn't even feel guilty about it. I knew I still loved my wife, and I also knew I was acting like a complete scumbag.

Then it was off to Dublin, London, Paris, Bern, Rome, Florence, Pisa, Barcelona and Amsterdam. As expected, while in Amsterdam, I did what any young American man, well not everyone, would do in the world's most famous adult playground. Nuff said. And yes, I was scum, again.

Chapter 7 -- New Job -- New Failure -- New Spiral

A few months after returning from Europe the News Gods suddenly smiled upon me once more. I was offered a job as a reporter for KNX Newsradio 1070, the legendary CBS-owned and operated radio station, located then in Hollywood. I felt bad leaving KHJ-TV so soon after they gave me time off to travel but I just couldn't pass up the opportunity. It was my first job in radio. The transition from TV to radio news was easy for me. By then I was no longer a rookie reporter, and I welcomed the fact that I would be covering stories with just a tape recorder as my "crew." And since the pay was better, what was not to love?

During my time at KHJ and KNX in the mid 70's and early 80's, I interviewed such luminaries as former California Governor and presidential hopeful Ronald Reagan, U.S. Senator Ted Kennedy, actors Farrah Fawcett, Jane Fonda, Sylvester Stallone, John Travolta and other famous movie stars. I also had the opportunity to interview the charismatic and memorable Harry Truman, the 83-year-old man who refused to leave his home and perished when nearby Mt. St. Helens erupted.

I spoke in person with former Beatle Ringo Starr when his Hollywood Hills home caught fire in 1979. I admit to being starstruck almost the entire time I spent working in Hollywood.

My favorite interview though, was Miss Lillian Carter, mother of the sitting president at the time. She was so cordial, with a fascinating wit and very proud of all her children. I was mesmerized by her joyful countenance.

Speaking of her son, President Jimmy Carter, it was my assignment once to cover a small part of one of his visits to Los Angeles. It was standard practice for us to witness and report every minute of the President's public appearances. Senior KNX reporters were covering the more salient aspects of the Chief Executive's visit while I was only tasked with describing the departure of the President outside the venue where he was speaking. It was expected to be a less-than-a-minute live report describing Mr. Carter's walking out of the building, waving to the throng of admirers, getting into his limousine and driving away. To my surprise, if not a little horror, he suddenly veered away from the limo and headed over to the crowd to shake hands and greet his well-wishers. The newsroom burst into my earpiece, "Stay with it. Stretch it out until he gets into the limo and leaves."

I was live on the air and really didn't know what to say. But from somewhere in my subconscious, I began recapping what I had learned about why the President was in town and why it mattered to Los Angeles and the nation. I described the individuals he was greeting, the actions of the Secret Service agents as they diligently protected the President during his unexpected and likely unplanned foray into the masses. I do not remember anything else I may have said during my report. I do recall my relief when Mr. Carter finally turned around, waved once more to the crowd and walked back to his limo and got in. I could finally breathe again, then sign off and send it back to the studio.

When I returned and entered the newsroom, I was

greeted by my news director and staff members who were applauding and shouting out congratulations for a job well done. They told me I had successfully and professionally described the totally unexpected scene for about five minutes without faltering once. My live report, which should have lasted about a minute, had seemed like an eternity to me. I was elated by the peer recognition, and proud of myself. Best of all, my Depression was nowhere to be seen.

It did not last long. I was covering the Rose Parade in Pasadena weeks later when I got a cryptic call from the assignments' editor. He said I needed to return to the station immediately. I was starting to ask him what the hell was going on and he interrupted me and said we would talk when I got back.

As I walked into the newsroom you could hear the proverbial pin drop as everyone suddenly got busy and quit talking. The assignments' editor stood up, gently reached for my arm and turned me around and began leading me down the hallway.

"Your brother Joe called and asked me to tell you that your sister is not expected to live much longer, and you need to get to the Gardena Hospital as soon as you can. Leave your tape recorder and notes with me and we'll pull the interviews you have from the parade," he said quietly. "We're all very sorry Phil, take as much time as you need and please be careful driving."

My oldest sister Leonore, or Nora, as we called her, had been suffering from Lupus for some time and had been hospitalized. She had suddenly taken a very serious turn for the worse, so her impending death was not a total surprise. I just didn't think it would be this soon. We were very close, she being the oldest and I the youngest of five siblings. Nora had always been very protective of me and I idolized her.

She managed to hang on for a couple of weeks, I think. I went back to work in the interim, but when the inevitable day finally came, I was not ready to say goodbye. Even though I expected it, I could not stop the spiral into my familiar well of Depression… again.

Phil Sisneros

Chapter 7.5 -- Goodbye L.A. and My Marriage

I do not recall how long it was before I went back to work after my sister died, but again I sucked it up as Coach Howell taught me in high school. Although my deep sadness made me feel like a zombie in a three-piece pinstripe suit, I concentrated on work during the week, trying to be a better reporter, a better news writer, a better all-around broadcast journalist.

Every day I started out thinking about how fortunate I was to be in Los Angeles reporting news. Shortly after noon though, it was as if a mentally painful darkness was slowly closing in on me. And unfortunately, by quitting time I was ready to ease my pain at the bar next door two or three nights a week before going home.

One would rightly think that with my broadcast career going so well for me, how could I possibly be unsatisfied? I learned later, too late in retrospect, that my Depression was robbing me of almost all the appreciation for the good things in my life. But as usual, I was able to mask my illness from my colleagues, friends and family. To be fair, if my family members knew, they did not talk about it to me.

During that time, I often found myself being angry and dissatisfied with just about everything. Looking back to my childhood for a moment; after one of her frequent complaint-ridden tirades I can remember my mother being scolded by my dad, "You wouldn't be happy if they hung you with a new rope!" His meaning is now clear to me.

Years later I learned that constant complaining was just one of the symptoms of Depression. I think my mother spent a lot of time at the bottom of the same well of despair that I would find myself in as I got older.

Circling back, my late nights, sullen behaviors, and overall apathy at home, took their toll on my short-lived marriage. As a result, about two years in, my wife suddenly confronted me in our living room and matter-of-factly told me that she was going on vacation, by herself, to Aruba. She then handed me a large manila envelope with a short note paper-clipped to the outside. It was her lawyer's contact information. She then politely asked me to have the divorce papers signed by the time she returned in a couple of weeks. I could only stand there slack jawed and unable to respond. Then, as she walked out the door, dragging two large suitcases, I envisioned and then heard the specter of ol' Mr. D waving goodbye to her and turning to me grinning and saying, "She's Hasta la Vista Baby!"

Luckily it was a Friday so of course I did a double somersault high dive into the Depression well and did not emerge until Sunday. And so, marriage number two went into the toilet. There I was, in Los Angeles with the best job I could ever hope to have at the time, but alone and more depressed than ever.

The divorce settlement left me with half the proceeds from the sale of our home and half the land we had purchased in Colorado. In retrospect I think I made a pretty good deal, she even agreed to keep the dogs until I could get settled somewhere.

That somewhere almost turned out to be Nicaragua.

There were opportunities for news people who spoke Spanish to become correspondents for American news networks as the political upheaval there was coming to a boiling point. I briefly thought about throwing in with the intrepid reporters and emulating Ernest Hemingway, who had famously immersed himself in several military conflicts. Nicaragua was a warzone. I was depressed and drank a lot, just like him, so maybe I could learn to write like him too, right? But it was just another one of my frequent fantasies. It was easy for me to plug into the make-believe whenever I felt like stepping away from the reality of the moment to distract myself. A coping mechanism? Probably.

Luckily for me, I quickly decided I did not want to die in a steamy jungle covering the guerilla warfare between the Sandinistas and the Contras. Besides, nobody could write like Hemingway so I pushed down my feelings of Depression and decided I would try to make the best out of what had become a pretty crappy situation.

Next, I did what any newly divorced young man would do in Southern California…move back to the beach. I found a new third floor, ocean facing apartment a block from the water with unobstructed views from my bedroom, living room and balcony. A bachelor's paradise, again. My daily commute to the radio station in Hollywood was almost always around forty-five minutes in the late 70's and early 80's, depending on freeway and surface street conditions. Not bad for a twenty-mile commute. Again, all was right with the world for me. Again, it didn't last.

I quickly discovered that the hot new nightclubs near the beach were all mostly within walking distance, so I became a frequent patron. I made new friends and was soon a Friday night party guy again who couldn't wait to get home from work, literally stripping off my tie and shirt the second I parked in the underground lot. Fortunately, my friend Bob was always up for a foray into the discos on the beach near our apartment building. Bob was my bachelor neighbor down the hall who was as lonely as me and was as happy as I was to have someone to commiserate with.

I met a lot of new ladies during this return to beach-bachelorhood. Although I had a brief semi-serious relationship, I was not in any condition in my head to commit to much of anything, much less another potential failure. So, I broke it off. The Depression was quickly dragging me down. I began to think I just needed to get out of L.A. and start over. I told my boss at KNX that I was thinking I needed a change of scenery. To his credit, knowing that I was recently divorced, I think he understood and offered to make a few calls and help me get transferred to another CBS station, WBBM in Chicago or KCBS in San Francisco. But I was already so depressed that I just asked him if he could give me a general letter of recommendation. I wasn't sure where to go or what to do, I just knew that Los Angeles was no longer where I wanted to be. Like several times before and more times to come, I was just running away from my Depression. I had learned that escaping the scene seemed to always help, if only for a while.

There was an older reporter and news anchor at KNX with whom I had become friendly. He knew I was from New Mexico and once told me he had been stationed at Kirtland Force Base in Albuquerque when he was in the U.S. Air Force in the old days. He said he always regretted not staying in New Mexico after he was discharged. With a big smile, he said "It is such a great place."

He knew I was not happy in L.A. anymore and asked me why I just didn't go back home? After some serious soul searching, I decided to do just that and go back to Albuquerque. I had not lined up a job, did not know where I'd live, or what I would actually do when I got there.

Chapter 8 -- Back to Burque & The Bean is Born

Larry, my best friend since childhood, lived in Albuquerque and arranged for us to become roommates in a rental house in the northeast heights. I moved in and got settled and then sent for my other best friend, Garbanzo. My ex-wife put my pup on a plane, and I picked him up at the Sunport. It took two days for the jet flight tranquilizers to wear off but Garbanzo was soon his old self and seemed happy to explore his new surroundings in Albuquerque.

I spent the first month back in New Mexico fishing and camping with Garbanzo, partying with old friends, and staring at the walls of my bedroom for long periods of time. I had plenty of money, mostly from my half of the divorce settlement so I was not actively looking for work. I was, and still am, a news junkie so my thoughts kept coming back to getting a job in TV news again.

Eventually I started knocking on doors at all the TV stations. Every news director I spoke with said they were very impressed by my experience, especially in Los Angeles. But all of them told me they were not hiring at the time for one reason or another. I got the sense though that they were asking themselves why a big city reporter would leave L.A. to come back to a small market like Albuquerque. I couldn't blame them, that is exactly one of the questions I was asking myself. Did I make a big mistake? Had I just thrown away a career that I had worked so hard to establish? What kind of idiot would give up Hollywood and the dream job of a lifetime? The answer was yes, yes, and me. I was that idiot.

I was morose, hopeless, an absolute failure, extreme regretful and suicidal. If there was ever a contest for one person to feel all these things at once, I would have won hands down. I was at a loss for what to do next. In the end, I reverted to my old remedies; drink, drugs, too casual sex, and sinking back into a deep Depression. I must have felt some comfort in all those things. Getting professional help was still not an option I seriously considered. It was once again, just plain stubbornness, shame, and the belief that I could beat this living hell by myself. And that kept me from seeking real help.

Then came a sliver of good news. Several media-biz friends told me they had heard that an Albuquerque radio station was looking for an experienced person to read the news in a new music format that was being put together. I quickly got my act together and set up an appointment to meet with the KOB-FM general manager. He briefly explained that KOB-FM was currently an automated station that played elevator music. The plan was to switch to an adult contemporary format featuring popular music of the time and call it 93.3 KOB-FM. The new station would have live air talent 24-7, including live newscasts. The live news content would be where I came into the plan.

We continued the usual job interview dance until he looked up from my resume and said, “Well, this certainly is impressive, but I’ve gotta ask, why would you come back here to work for a salary that, I can tell you now, is a great deal less that what you were making in LA?”

“I was born and raised here, my folks are getting older,

I was sick of big city life, and I just missed being home," I replied. The money was not a big factor for me, but I did not say so then.

"It's not completely up to me, our new program director will make the final decision," the GM said. "Steve Hatley is his name, and he will call you so you two can set up a meeting."

Steve Hatley and I met for the first time at a local Albuquerque Chinese restaurant to have lunch and discuss what my job would entail if I was hired. I remember being immediately impressed with his demeanor, sense of humor, and knowledge of the music radio world, even if at the time I didn't know much about music other than what I liked to hear. He asked me about my news experience and if I thought I could adapt to a more humorous laid-back approach and style. I don't remember what it was, but I must have said something funny in reply because he burst out laughing and said he thought we were going to have a lot of fun. I got the job. I would be Steve's sidekick and partner who read the news and participated in a new two-man entertainment radio morning show.

Steve was not the kind of guy to brag about himself, but I soon learned that he had been a highly accomplished 'jock' in several major radio markets around the country. His vast knowledge of music, quick wit and subtle sarcasm coupled with an incredibly listenable deep voice and easy delivery would make him instantly popular on Albuquerque radio. I was very lucky to be paired with such a multi-talented man.

We then discussed how our new morning show would work. Things like where the newscasts would be placed during each hour, the content and duration of each newscast, and the roles Steve and I would play during the rest of each hour on the air. Steve would handle all the music flow with regular commentary by me concerning certain songs and broader observations and thoughts about world and local events. We would interview or just talk to people on the air. The show would be like a TV talk show with great music, cash giveaways, huge-prize contests, and newscasts. And since I was a New Mexico native, I would provide local 'color,' if you will. And also, since I was Hispanic, that color would later include a lot of brown. It was a role that I would enjoy and exploit in every way I could.

Steve definitely had the harder part of this pairing. In addition to many other duties, not only did he have to lead the morning show, but he was also responsible for choosing the station's music, the commercial placement format, contest and promotion planning, all the things that make a morning radio show successful. Steve also had the unenviable job of supervising the diverse, individually multifaceted, multitalented and kind of crazy group of on-air talent. Sometimes it was like herding cats. It was just the kind of gang I wanted to be in.

93 KOB-FM was owned by a large media corporation based out of Minnesota when I first became The Bean on the radio. Before I took the moniker though, the company sent Steve and me to Minneapolis to hang out with their wildly popular morning show guys on (KS95) KSTP-FM to get advice on how to structure our new show back in Albuquerque. The dynamic duo, Chuck Knapp and Michael Wegner, a/k/a, *Knapp and Donuts* ruled the airwaves in Minneapolis in the 80's and we would style our yet-to-be-named morning program after theirs. As we were driving back to our hotel after a late-into-the-evening party uh…meeting with these

guys, Steve suddenly blurted out, "So what the hell are we gonna call our show?"

Like a verbal tennis match it was 'The Steve and Phil Show', 'Hatley and Sisneros', etc., etc., etc. Nothing either one of us came up with sounded right. We got quiet and just kept driving, clearly frustrated that we could not conjure a name that was funny, catchy, and memorable. The eastern sky was beginning to lighten up with the first hints of dawn as we slogged down the freeway when I visualized a scene from the 1974 buddy cop action movie Freebie and the Bean. I slammed my hand on the dashboard and spouted, "I got it, I got it man! You remember that movie, Freebie and the Bean? The one with Alan Arkin and James Caan where they play nut job detective partners who screw up all the time but still win the day? We could call ourselves Stevie and The Bean!"

"Hummm," he mused. "I like it but, you being Hispanic, would calling yourself a bean go over well in a big Hispanic demographic in Albuquerque?" I replied, "Why not? I AM a Mexican-American who loves to eat beans by the way. And I have a dog named Garbanzo for chrissakes, you know, as in garbanzo *beans*? It's perfect. I'm a beaner Steve. I'm born and raised in New Mexico and damned proud of it. I can offer that homeboy perspective like no one else can. On top of that, I can read and write news like a Chicano Cronkite!"

And so, I became The Bean, Beans, Mr. Beans, or El Frijole, depending on who you talked with. I was happier than two dead birds in the sun. My Depression was nowhere to be seen, I felt great, I was excited about my life again and proud to be a part of building a new radio station from the ground up. For a change, like one of the new station's slogans said, my life was 'Always Sunny.' I paid no attention to the dark clouds starting to build over the nearby Sandia Mountains.

The new 93.3 KOB-FM took off like a rocket from White Sands Missile Range. It was not long after launching that we went to the top of the ratings on Albuquerque-area radio. The Stevie and The Bean morning show led the way behind a great marketing plan that included billboards with our caricatured faces, coffee mugs, big soft drink cups, and posters. We were even asked to be grand marshals for a parade. Life could not get any better for me.

Over the next couple of years, we were part of numerous radio publicity stunts that usually got us in trouble with our boss or some public official. We received industry accolades and we enjoyed immense popularity with our listeners. I absolutely ate it all up. I could barely sleep most nights because I couldn't wait to drive to work at 4:30 in the morning.

In those early days we did not do a lot of show prep, as it was called in the biz. We preferred to mostly wing it as we poured out our creative juices to discuss current events and play off each other on a daily basis. There were not many topics that we could not find humor in, and yes, sometimes we stretched the limits of propriety.

Like I had done in Los Angeles a few years before, we had occasion to interview the famous and near famous. We did a live interview in studio with nationally popular psychic Sylvia Browne, a hit and miss psychic who had appeared on The Larry King Show and other prominent talk shows. We learned later that very few of her predictions ever came true. I can't remember any of them she made in our interview although ironically, many believe that she predicted the 2020 COVID outbreak, seven years after her death.

We also did lots and lots of community events. In 1983 we served as honorary hosts for the local Super Walk for

March of Dimes to combat birth defects. We rallied hundreds of listeners to participate and raised thousands of dollars.

Being that I was home grown, Steve was born in Oklahoma, it was easy for me to talk about things that were part of New Mexico culture and history. For example, having been born in Española, I spoke about the legend of La Llorona, a ghostly figure of a woman who haunted the ditches and riverbanks in New Mexico after allegedly drowning her children because she could not afford to raise them.

We talked about Mexican cuisine like the arduous process of making tamales, the uniquely New Mexican practice of roasting green chile farmed only in the Land of Enchantment, eating the Mexican delicacy menudo, a dish made from boiled cow stomach and red chile. We promoted events like the Fiestas de Santa Fe that celebrated the reconquest of Santa Fe by those Spaniards in 1692 after the 1680 revolt by the local Pueblo Indians. The fiestas included the annual burning of Zozobra or Old Man Gloom, a fifty-foot marionette stuffed with notes from the locals of all their worries and concerns and then torched sending all our cares up in smoke. Kind of like Burning Man without the LSD. It is one of the oldest such celebrations in the country, dating back to the early 1700s.

I talked about riding the historic Cumbres and Toltec railroad in Chama, built in the late 1800s and the fact that I glowed in the dark because I had been raised in Los Alamos. Steve soon started calling me the Clown Prince of Española (a town a little northwest of Santa Fe where I was born and the butt of jokes for many New Mexicans) on the air. It was a title I carried with great pride. Things were going so well, it was like I had hit the radio jackpot and another career milestone.

Chapter 9 -- The Wrath of Mom Continues

Shortly after I returned home to New Mexico, my parents heath began to deteriorate, and I was able to visit with my mom and dad in their home more often. As I got older our mother/son relationship, slowly but surely, began to deteriorate. In her golden years she had a stroke and she became exceedingly acerbic. Given her medical/mental condition maybe I should have been more forgiving but after a lifetime of being put down I just couldn't laugh it off anymore. It was easier for me to just brood and be sad than get into an argument with her.

Not too long after her stroke, Dad began a quick slide into dementia. Their home in Los Alamos was no longer safe for them because it was a two-story apartment and the stairs could have been deadly. So, my oldest brother Joe and his life partner Jerry, who lived in California, purchased a house for my parents in Albuquerque in hopes they could live out their lives in a safer, one-story home. They also paid for live-in help to cook, clean, and assist Mom and Dad with pretty much everything. The alternating young female caregivers, mostly from Mexico, were OK with bathing my mother and assisting in her toileting needs but they were too uncomfortable doing the same for my dad.

In the beginning, Junior and I were taking turns checking in on the folks every day. However, my brother said he could not bring himself to help Dad with showering, grooming and using the toilet when Pops needed assistance. My bro was squeamish that way, he always had been. Since there was nobody else to do that, those duties fell to me. Nothing in a man's life can prepare him for wiping and washing his own father's butt, shaving him and combing his hair.

Meanwhile, Mom frequently began my visits by immediately launching into complaints about nearly everything I was doing on behalf of my parents. When I bought groceries, she would grouse that I got the wrong brand of green beans, or I forgot to get the kind of candy she liked. If I cooked lunch or dinner, the food didn't taste right. By then I was also managing my folks' finances so of course, she believed I was stealing her money.

Nothing I was doing was good enough for her. She would always say, "When my Chappie comes from California, he'll take care of everything, you won't have to bother." Chappie is what she called my oldest brother Joe, who made the trip from Los Angeles about once a month to visit my parents. When Joe arrived, she smiled from ear to ear and all was right in her world until he had to go back home. Afterward, dear ol' Mom seldom missed a chance to tell Junior and me that, unlike brother Joe, we "weren't worth a shit."

Not surprisingly, I dreaded my daily visits. Junior eventually just stopped going to see the folks. At first, I was pissed but then I realized what a toll it was taking on him emotionally, so I just added another shovel-full of sand and rocks to my Depression backpack and carried on. Most days I would go home afterward, pour a glass of whiskey, put on some music, and stare at the walls. Depression squeezed my soul like a steel vise.

My father was first to require 24/7 care. We chose a

nursing home for him which was not far away from their home. I think Joe and maybe my sister Jennie were also there on the day my dad was admitted. Before he got really sick, Dad would frequently ask me to promise never to put him in a nursing home. I broke that promise and I have felt guilty ever since, even though I know it was the best thing we could do for him at the time. The day he was admitted, it was gut wrenching for me to watch the nursing home staff wheel him off to his room.

Unless I was very sick or had a work-related thing, I visited my Pops every day after I was off the air. As I walked through the lobby toward his room, I'd wipe the sadness from my face and replace it with a smile, and as I entered his room, I would cheerily ask, "Hey Dad! How'ya doin' today?" Sometimes he would simply reply, "OK," and sometimes he would give me a vacant look and say nothing. So, I would start talking about the latest news concerning Mom, how other family members were faring, my job, the weather, any fucking thing I could think of to keep myself from melting down in front of him. It felt like some kind of beast was ripping my heart out of my chest and swallowing it before my eyes.

Dad liked to hear Mexican music, so I purchased small radios for him, repeatedly. Because his motor skills were quickly deteriorating, he invariably knocked them off the shelf next to his bed while trying to turn them on or off and, of course, they shattered on the floor. He would do the same thing with multiple electric shavers I bought for him. Even though I shaved him every couple of days, sometimes he wanted to do it himself.

One day as I entered his room, I saw another shaver in pieces on the floor next to his bed. I lost it. As I picked up the remains, I started yelling at my dad for being so clumsy and not waiting for me to shave him. I looked up at him from where I was picking up the pieces and he was looking at me with tears in his eyes, mumbling that he was sorry and pleading with me to not be mad at him. I immediately stood up, grabbed his hand and through my own tears, apologized and said I would bring him a new shaver tomorrow. I was horrified by what I had just done. I do not think I had ever been so disgusted with myself, or more depressed. I wanted to die.

But the next day I continued to be The Bean on the radio. Once again, I was that wise-cracking, always laughing, fun-loving guy who didn't have a care in the world. I gave it my best shot anyway. But when I switched off the microphone my real world fell over me like a heavy black tear-soaked blanket. The daily dread set in as I drove to the nursing homes to visit my folks. By then the Bastard Monkey had definitely taken up permanent residence in my head and on my back. The idea of getting professional help was still not something I felt I could do.

Then, while I was still coming to terms with having to sentence my dad to the nursing home, my mother reached the point physically where she too was placed in a nursing facility. Home care was no longer an option so once again arrangements were made for her long-term care. After that, my Depression went into hyper-drive and if there was a substance to abuse, I would. Adding to my perceived bucket of turds, my mother's nursing home was a separate one, at Dad's request. He said he too had had enough of my mother and did not want to be at the same place. That made me laugh but I could relate. We never told her what he said.

Almost immediately after settling in at the nursing home, Mom continued her flamethrower verbal assaults on me and almost anyone else nearby. For various reasons, none of which I remember, she was transferred to at least two other care facilities before what turned out to be her last. And just as I had come to dread my daily visits to my parents' home before they were placed in nursing facilities, I now dreaded my trips to see them in their new homes. As emotionally hard as it was to see Dad, it was a piece of cake compared to visiting Mom.

Before I passed through the glass doors at her nursing home entrance, I frequently stopped to look at my reflection to make sure my hair was combed, my clothes weren't rumpled, and I had a big smile on my face. One day I walked in during lunch time. Before I could even greet her, my mother blurted out, "Phillip, you're getting too fat again. That shirt doesn't look like it was ironed, and I thought you were coming earlier!" The lady sitting next to her, who was her roommate, said, "Alice! You shouldn't talk to your son like that. He came here to see you!"

I stopped in my tracks, shook my head in dejection then turned around and walked away. Back in my truck, I stared at the steering wheel and just crumbled. I thought, geez, here I am a grown man crying because my mom said something mean to me. I was pissed at myself, and I felt like a wimp. I went straight to some friends' home and drank half a bottle of their Scotch while I spilled out my bruised feelings.

Chapter 10 -- Dark Clouds Drift Down Again

Less than two years into the Stevie and The Bean saga, I slowly began slipping back into that familiar darkness. My ego could have entered the annual International Balloon Fiesta held every October in Albuquerque as a Special Shape. My alcohol and substance abuse increased, mood swings became my normal, and somehow, I became disenchanted with the Land of Enchantment. I really don't remember if the Depression was affecting my work on the show but off-air I was moody and I complained about this or that. I know Steve noticed the change. He did not pull any punches and told me, "If you're so unhappy with this, maybe you should just do something else."

Even though the ensuing months are fuzzy now, I must have managed to get my act together again. The morning show was in high gear, the other time slots were sizzling and our overall ratings were skyrocketing. 93 KOB-FM even made the cover of Broadcasting Magazine, the national news journal for the broadcasting industry. The headline read; *New Mexico's Number One Music Station...Again.*

Then the bottom fell out of my world at the end of February 1984. Steve Hatley was killed in a motorcycle accident. Steve and I had just finished a motorcycle safety and training course in preparation for a station-sponsored motorcycle cross-country promotion where we would do live broadcasts from the road. Steve was on his way home when he somehow collided with at least one vehicle as he crossed the old Alameda Bridge in northwest Albuquerque.

In an instant, Steve's wife Linda, who was pregnant, became a widow. His sudden death was even more tragic in that he never got to meet his new son, who was born shortly after his death. Obviously, Steve's passing was an unfathomable and enormous loss for his family. My own loss paled in comparison to theirs, but it was no less life changing.

Over the years, Steve and I developed a close personal and working friendship. On the personal level we shared a lot of the same interests like fishing and shooting firearms and cars. Working as a team on the radio was easy because we each had outgoing personalities and a shared sense of humor. We had a great chemistry together on air, we could finish each other's thoughts and even sentences. We laughed and poked fun at each other and got along like two guys who had known each other for years. We also shared information about personal problems and past events that shaped our lives. I shared a lot of things with Steve, except my Depression and how it was affecting my life.

Suddenly, the Stevie and The Bean morning show was no more. I was numb and unable to think clearly; barely able to talk to anyone. It was a maelstrom of confusion, emotions, concerned well-wishers, even requests for comment by local news media. I remember parts of the funeral, especially looking over at Linda and wondering what she was going to do now. I felt guilty for wondering what *I* was going to do too. I stood before the other mourners and tried to say something appropriate. To this day I do not remember my words. I also cannot recall how long I was off work before I returned to the air at the station. When I finally pushed the microphone ON button, I was terrified and not sure if I could handle the non-stop flood of calls from saddened and shocked listeners. In addition to losing Steve, for me it was truly ‘the day the music died.’

Of course I dove headfirst into Depression. This time, instead of just treading water in that damned hole, I kept slipping under the surface. For the first time since coming to the radio station, thoughts of suicide floated in and out of my mind. The Bastard was drowning me by putting a giant suicidal monkey on my back. And not just any simian, this was King Kong. I think my mind imploded, yet I confided in no one and eventually managed to daily put on the happy face and demeanor of The Bean, death monkey notwithstanding.

I’m told the station arranged for a jock from another time slot to join me on the morning show until a permanent replacement for Steve could be hired but to this day, I remember very little of that time period or how long it was. Still, I thought I could drink and drug myself out of the depths and simultaneously keep going on the radio. Mr. Beans, that Chicano clown, continued. Maybe it was the work, along with the support of people who listened to the show, that kept me coming back to the studio every morning and pressing the mic ON button, or maybe I just thought it was what Steve Hatley would have wanted me to do. I heard him in my headphones every morning.

Eventually, a new guy was hired to be the KOB-FM program director and co-host of the morning show. The Jay and The Bean era began. We were good together and our ratings were good too. I continued to wear the mask and no one, not even my new partner, knew about my Depression.

At first, I didn't want to continue being The Bean. I figured that Stevie and The Bean was a once in a lifetime pairing that couldn't and shouldn't be duplicated. I suppose that I experienced the well-known stages of grief; Denial, Anger, Bargaining, Depression, and Acceptance. My Depression was the strongest emotion, resulting in the first time that I really thought I couldn't come back from my sadness. It was the first time in my life that I was scared about my thoughts of suicide. I believed it was the only way to end my pain, and I was afraid I would end my own life. To this day, I can't explain why I didn't take my own life or why I decided to stay on at the radio station. I guess the Universe had different plans for me and I just took things one day at a time.

I was a different person when I got home every day after the show then. Nothing seemed funny to me, and I did not feel like joking about anything. That person thought cocaine and whiskey would make him a new man, and that new guy would snap out of it and climb out of that damned Depression well. I continued to selfishly think I might be better off if I was not here anymore. Subconsciously, I knew I was out of control and needed help, but I could not find the courage to ask for it.

Somehow, I managed to keep a girlfriend for several years during that time. I never admitted my Depression to her as I treaded water and sank below the surface at times. I was constantly amazed that one woman, (DV), would stay with me longer than either of my two marriages lasted. I felt that I didn't deserve a stable relationship and tried my best to fuck it all up. I eventually succeeded and we broke up.

Meanwhile, I continued the charade at work. The Bean was 'Always Sunny' and I genuinely believed I could help ordinary people feel good about their lives as they drove to work and maybe put a smile on their faces. Sometimes I even felt like I had beaten the Depression and could see some light ahead. In retrospect, I wish I could have taken some of my on-air persona's optimism and applied it to my real life.

Then, as if following a recurring script, I fell in love again before the ashes had cooled from my last failure. I constantly professed my undying affection for this new woman until she at last told me she loved me too. We quickly planned to move in together and get married. I was understandably aglow with happiness; we even got the marriage license. But those plans and my elation were short lived. Fortunately for her, before any of that could happen, she came to her senses and unceremoniously kicked me to the curb. (KF) had rightly saved herself from boarding the Titanic that was my life.

This break up hit me harder than any previous one for some reason. I really thought this relationship would be the one that lasted forever and might finally float me up and out of the well of Depression. I know now that it was an unreasonable, if not downright stupid expectation.

One Saturday night, sitting around my kitchen table at home, a couple of friends and I were drinkin' an snortin' like bachelors do when they tire of the nightclub scene. The three of us were well into recreational incoherency while solving the problems of the world when I recounted my recent heartbreak. At some point I said I was so depressed over the breakup that I did not want to live without her and was thinking about suicide. My good friend (MS) suddenly backhanded me so hard I nearly fell over backward out of my chair, spilled my drink too, damn it.

"You stupid son of a bitch!," he yelled. "No woman is worth killing yourself over! Don't ever let me hear you say that again!" He never knew it but he saved my life that night. I buried the notion as deep as I could and decided to concentrate on the morning show.

That helped me stay above water for several years and through a series of new morning show partners and girlfriends. It was Jay and The Bean, Mikey and The Bean, Biondi and The Bean, Birdman and The Bean, and lastly, John and The Bean. If any of them knew how desperately unhappy I was, no one ever let on.

Somewhere in that mix I managed to fall in love yet again! I know, some of you must be thinking that this guy doesn't even know what love is. I cannot disagree. I'm not sure I understand love now. Anyway, I fell hard for a longtime friend with whom I never expected to have such feelings. Long story short, everything was great between us until it wasn't. (EV) apparently realized she wanted to steer her life in a different direction and unfortunately for me, that path did not include me.

If you had looked into the dictionary, under the words 'unrequited love' at that time, you would have found my dumb face. Shattered, that's a good word to describe my reaction at the time. She could not or would not tell me why she had so suddenly ended our relationship. I played the blame game with myself, as usual. Did I not make it clear that I was in love with her? Did I do something that was a red line for her? Was it just me as a person that made her go away?

Once again, I packed my mental baggage and jumped headfirst into that oh-so-familiar hole of Depression. Bonnie Raitt's 'I Can't Make You Love Me' became the song I could not quit listening to, over and over. To this day, hearing the song still hurts my heart. A short time later, I learned that (EV) had been diagnosed with a cancer that later took her life. (EV) never told me why she had walked away from our relationship. I suspect she knew about the cancer before she broke up with me. Maybe she was trying to save me from the heartbreak of watching her suffer? I do not know if I will ever put her death behind me. As the saying goes, you never forget, you just learn to live with it.

You are not paying attention if you have not picked up on the fact that most of my Depression episodes involved women. None of them were at fault really. In truth, I know it was me that caused every relationship to crash and burn.

Chapter 11-- Dog Dies, Job Dies, Was I Next?

At the time, I think I was partnered on the radio with Mike (Mikey) Phillips when I lost another big part of my life. After almost thirteen years with me through thick and thin, I finally had to say goodbye to my best friend and companion, my wonderful dog Garbanzo. I talked about him so often that listeners felt like they knew him. There are so many stories about our adventures together, but I will leave them for another telling somewhere down the line someday. Quite frankly, even after all these years, it still hurts to discuss his death.

But it was because of him that I met the woman to whom I am still married to as of this writing. Debbie was a ‘dog nurse’ at the animal clinic where I eventually took Garbanzo after he first got sick. She looked after him and would let me in to see him on weekends when the clinic was closed. Despite the good care he received, Garbanzo soon died. He was about 13 years old. A big part of me died too. After my puppy passed, Deb and I started dating. I think my buddy knew I needed to be with someone like her. I have always believed that before he died, Garbanzo told me Debbie was the one.

By this time I had moved on to yet another partner, Joe Biondi. I asked Debbie to marry me and we flew to Hawaii where we wed on the beach leaving Joe behind to handle the show. I did still do live cut ins for the show from my wedding. I was in my late 30's, when the idea came to me to start a group of dancing fat guys called the Chunkendales. The famous male striptease act, The Chippendales, was coming to Albuquerque as part of their national tour in the early 1990's. I posed these questions to our female listeners, "Would you be interested in seeing a group of half-naked guys without chiseled physiques or professional dancing abilities do a striptease act?" and "What if these guys were a little overweight and nowhere as good looking or talented as the Chippendales?"

The majority of women who called into the station said they would love to see such an act made up of local everyday guys. A few callers said no, the idea was repulsive. I went with the yes callers. I weighed about 240 pounds at the time so I immediately went on the air looking for men weighing about that or more who wanted to strip for a bunch of enthusiastic women. The phones lit up instantly and within minutes I had five guys who volunteered. Since we were all kinda chunky, I called the group The Chunkendales, deliberately to make fun of and parody the Chippendales.

We were an instant success and performed a number of charity events in Albuquerque before hundreds of crazed women who unabashedly stuffed dollar bills into our G-strings. Then I got a call from People Magazine. The resulting article launched overnight coverage from national newspapers and requests to appear on national TV talk shows. The Sally Jessey Raphael show flew the whole group to New York where we performed on her program. Luckily my new wife had a great sense of humor and had no objections to me stripping before a national audience.

Unfortunately, lawyers for The Chippendales contacted the

radio station and threatened the company with a Cease-and-Desist Order if the company did not immediately stop sponsoring the Chunkendales. I had to leave the group, but the guys struck out on their own and performed more local charity events and even did the Montel Williams nationally syndicated tv show in Hollywood.

My thoughts of committing suicide came and went. I was able to put my self-harm thoughts in what I now imagine to have been something like a clear locked box. And I could put that box on a shelf in the back of my mind for a time.

But every so often I found myself looking at the box and seeing a snarling grotesque creature inside. Sometimes it escaped the box, sending me for another dip in the D-well. Each time, this suicide monster seemed more difficult to corral and lock up again.

Despite my mental difficulties, Debbie and I managed to gather enough funding to start building our dream home in the mountains of northern New Mexico at Heron Lake. We robbed Peter to pay Paul and juggled finances to pay for the initial homesite infrastructure. Then we took out a large home loan to complete the project. As a result, we now had two mortgages to pay. My plan was to sell our home in Rio Rancho and begin broadcasting my part of the radio show remotely from the lake house. Station management was initially receptive to my plan and promised to work out the details with me in the coming months.

But before that could happen, my planned lake-house of cards suddenly collapsed when I was summarily fired by KOB-FM. I had been told that I would have to accept a fifty percent reduction in pay and essentially train a new morning show personality to take my place. And they told me I would become a third wheel accessory for the show, and I was forbidden to discuss what was happening with the already selected new morning show talent that they were going to hire to replace me. So of course, I immediately met with the new person and told them exactly what was going on. To their credit, this person then declined the station's offer to replace me and told them why. That's when all hell broke loose and the current general manager almost had a stroke in front of me when he fired me. He even admitted that he had never been so angry in his life as he ordered me out of the building immediately.

Complete shock does not come close to describing my reaction to being kicked out on my butt. Coming barely months after I had signed a new contract, I could not comprehend what had just occurred. And, under that so-called legal agreement, I was also not allowed to seek employment at another radio station for a very long time. It is called a non-compete clause in a contract. So essentially, I had lost the right to make a living in broadcasting in the wider Albuquerque area. That left me with two mortgages and no job. Funny how some parts of a legal contract are enforceable, but others are not. It's like Vegas, the House always wins. But I was not going to go 'gentle into that good night,' as written by the poet Dylan Thomas. It's fitting that the poem is about death.

I'll spare you the details of the long and costly court battle that ensued, get it? (en-SUED). I'm surprised I can joke about it now. Suffice it to say that we lost our newly built home at Heron Lake and decimated my 401K retirement plan because I took money out of it to pay for legal fees. By the way, I still had to pay it back and pay a 10% penalty plus income taxes, or something like that. In any case, the financial and mental health losses were devastating, and I felt so betrayed after spending more than twenty years serving as a cash cow for the station. I wasn't even allowed to say goodbye to the loyal listeners. I became a very angry man. But rather than rag on the station and describe the corporate fucking I received, I would rather tell you about what this did to my Depression and how I dealt with it or didn't.

In the weeks after my personal Armageddon, all I could think about again was checking out of planet Earth. My shock and sadness had suddenly gone supernova but watching my wife struggle with her own grief of losing our dream mountain home pulverized me. I was so distraught that I temporarily lost the ability to smell or taste. As a result, I almost quit eating entirely and dropped more than twenty pounds in a very short time. I was too fat anyway so that part was probably good for me, right?

I soon concluded that I could not and would not continue to live with this heart grinding loss. I went so far as to choose the pistol I would use, where I would do it so as not to cause a mess, and what I would write in the note I would leave behind. But somehow, I could not act upon my plan. I cannot explain to you why I failed to take my own life because I don't really know. Perhaps it was my tendency to over-think and attempt to rationalize every major decision I have ever made. In this case, that habit likely saved me from myself.

Clearly, I needed professional help at that point, but still I resisted the idea. I believed that if I told a therapist how I was feeling they would be obligated to report that to the Suicides-R-Us agency and the guys in white uniforms would show up and cart me off to a rubber room. So again, I decided to self-medicate and try to find my own way out of the well.

I was spiraling downward and drowning in my own tears. Yeah, hard as it is to admit for a macho man, I cried nearly every day until I exhausted myself and fell asleep.

Some people sleep a lot when they are depressed and consider suicide, hoping to never wake up. But I stayed alive, miserable beyond measure, but I stayed alive.

As the months went by, with help of friends and Deb's salary, we kept afloat. One friend temporarily hired me to do odd jobs around his office building. Then I took a job at the local Radio Disney station, again thanks to some friends. I could not be on the air due to the non-compete clause in my old KOB-FM piece of crap contract. Remember, they could fire me and prevent me from working as an on-air talent too. But I could be a radio commercial time salesman, so I did that. And I was allowed, under that same toilet paper contract to perform the Chicken Dance with little kids at public appearances for the Disney radio station.

At first, I was embarrassed by how low I had sunk professionally. I mean, I went from a long-time top-rated radio personality to a Mickey Mouse job, literally. Even though my Depression had gutted my self-esteem and taken me to the precipice, seeing the smiles on kids' faces when our Disney Cast performed made me feel good. Every day was a little bit better and soon the thoughts of ending it all faded, at least for a while.

Chapter 12 -- Politics, A New Path

Then good fortune, friends and perhaps divine intervention, led me to one of the best jobs I have ever had outside of broadcasting. I say divine intervention because the man who recommended me for the job later became a top religious leader.

Because of that recommendation, Dr. Gary King, of the famous New Mexico political/ranching family, hired me to be communications director for his campaign for state attorney general. Luckily for me, he was also a fan of The Bean on the radio and apparently knew of my experience as a journalist. I was so grateful and excited to transition to a new career working for one of the most respected men in New Mexico politics. Of course, Gary was elected and I spent the next eight years on his staff. For most of that time my Depression mostly went underground. Occasionally it would raise its nasty head but by then I was an expert at masking the outward signs and no one was aware.

But at the end of those eight years, I again did not have a job. The Depression made a comeback as I found myself sucking water in the D-well. Another good friend, (JF), then hired me for a short stint as communications/public relations director for his small software company. He had experience dealing with people close to him who suffered Depression so he was more than tolerant and understanding when my illness made it difficult to do my job.

A quick note here to readers. I am one of the people with Depression who had a very difficult time referring to my mental health condition as an illness. Perhaps it was because of the stigma that I mentioned earlier in this saga; my reluctance to admit to myself that I had Depression. The long-held belief that I alone could manage it or maybe it was just male vanity that kept me from assigning a medical term to what I was experiencing. It took me a while, but I finally learned to call it an illness. And it took me a little while longer to be able to talk to people about being Depressed for most of my life and not feel embarrassed or uncomfortable. I encourage you to be honest with yourself and the people around you if you suffer from this illness.

I next took a temporary job with the Bernalillo County district attorney's office as a public information officer in 2016. It was understood that the position was only for the last year of the DA's longtime term in office. During that time, amongst the usual white collar and non-violent offenses, I sometimes was exposed to the devastation caused by evil, murderous criminals. Before, as a journalist, I had regularly reported on gory heinous crimes, natural disasters, plane crashes, and countless examples of Man's inhumanity to Man.

But usually after my report, I moved on to the next story and did not often dwell on the horrible carnage and criminal viciousness. But that was not an option in this job. Working with prosecutors to constantly keep the public informed through the news media required constant immersion and updating of the facts in the seemingly never-ending stream of gore and disgusting criminal cases. I have deep respect for the lawyers who wade daily into that cesspool of depraved criminal activity. It got to me. The case that finally did it was the 2016 murder and dismemberment of a ten-year-old girl named Victoria Martens. Her own mother and two of her drug addict friends were convicted in connection with her death.

After a year, it was time for me to leave as agreed upon. Even though I was not yet old enough to receive full Social Security benefits, I decided to retire. Like a burnt T-bone, I was done.

One of the words I can use to describe why I so often couldn't enjoy my successes in my professional and private life…DOUBT. When I look back on my life, DOUBT was always there.

When I was hired at the TV station in Albuquerque, I was elated and proud that my previous performance as a college intern was apparently recognized and the job was a reward. However, soon after starting, I would be at home lying in bed thinking about why I got the job. Was it because I earned it? Was it because I was a fresh brown face that met some diversity requirement or public relations claim? Was my job performance up to par, or was I given a pass because I was a minority? The thoughts made me sad and afraid that my new career was just a bubble that could burst at any time. Eventually, I was able to push down most of the negative thoughts and enjoy my successes on a daily basis. Many years later I learned that self-doubt is a common symptom of Depression.

After moving to Phoenix for a new TV news job I discovered the self-doubts were still with me, but they were manageable. Then a new mental goblin appeared. During my off time at home, I began experiencing periods when I found myself staring at a wall or the ceiling while feeling lonely, sad, and angry at myself for screwing up my first marriage. Other unrelated thoughts and images appeared in my head too. None of the thoughts were positive or happy.

I felt disconnected from everything and very alone. The thoughts kept circling me as though I was stuck, not moving, in the middle of a merry go round while the horses went by, over and over again. These bouts of staring could last anywhere from ten minutes to an hour or more. Although I was usually awake, sometimes I fell asleep while staring and ruminating. Often times after one of these events I would head to our local watering hole and knock back a few beers to distract myself from thinking about what had just happened. Other times, for the same reason, I used cocaine, marijuana, and alcohol. I did this mostly with friends but occasionally I preferred to be by myself.

This cause and effect behavior persisted when my job took me to California. So many good things happened to me personally and professionally, yet I couldn't always appreciate my good fortune. It was as if some of those feel-good endorphins one gets from success got sucked into the famous La Brea Tar Pits in Los Angeles. I literally got mad at myself for not being happy! As a result, I self-medicated to help ease the pain.

Then, a new behavior emerged. I started putting up an air of false bravado in front of news gathering colleagues, especially those who represented direct competitors. I didn't want to be seen as a novice newcomer to the big leagues. I believed if I looked and acted tough, I would be more easily accepted by the gang.

In the late 70s and early 80s, a major breaking news event in LA instantly attracted a horde of reporters and photographers that resembled piranhas savagely competing for the meat of the story. Usually, some official in charge would appear to make a statement to the press. The strongest and loudest broadcast crews fought their way to the front in hopes of getting that coveted "sound bite" that would lead the evening news. I wanted to be among them, so my photographer and sound man physically shoved me from behind through the herd like the famous Philadelphia Eagles' "Tush Push" football play. But I didn't like acting tough, it felt boorish and wrong, it wasn't me. After work, I thought three shots of scotch and a few beers would wash away the guilt from my bad behavior. This was my life then. This was my Depression.

When I finally came back to Albuquerque and began a new life chapter as The Bean on the radio, my sullenness, sadness, reckless and self-destructive choices had become normal to me. To my friends, family and coworkers, my demeanor and actions apparently didn't raise any red flags. I had become so skilled at masking my internal pain that nobody ever brought it up to me. At times I thought maybe I had imagined it all, from childhood to adulthood. However, in recent years I told my brother and sister about my struggles. I came clean to a few friends as well. All of them were surprised and empathetic. I know it was therapy that helped me reveal my Depression. Openness about my illness continues to be part of my continuing therapy. Hell, I even wrote a book about it!

Chapter 13 -- Retirement Almost Kills Me

My Depression ebbed and flowed as I spent my newfound retirement time fishing, hunting, camping and doing projects around the house that I had never before had the time to tackle. I finished most of the projects in less than a year. Uncharacteristically for me, I gradually lost interest in the fishing trips and being outdoors in general. And whatever recreational plans I may have thought about were put on hold, indefinitely. I didn't realize it then, but Depression can make you lose interest in a lot of things.

What I had overlooked was the fact that my wife was still working and had no plans to retire any time soon. She loves her job as a Registered Veterinary Technician and even after 45 years, she was not ready to say goodbye to all those dogs and cats that needed help. So here I was ready to rock retirement, but my wife was not. At first, I thought, no problem. There are tons of things I can do by myself. I decided that I would just keep busy until we could start doing things together, but as it turned out, that didn't happen very often.

Instead, I slept a lot during the day. I stared at the TV for hours, not caring what was on. I stopped reading, which is one of my favorite pastimes. Within months of retiring, I had absolutely nothing to do. The daily rigors and responsibilities of a job are what kept me relatively sane over the years but now, with no job to go to every day, the Genie of Depression explodes like the atomic bomb over Nagasaki. And as the idiom asserts, "you can't put the genie back in the bottle."

I spoke very little to anyone, even family. I was angry about almost everything and everybody. Inwardly, I felt like I didn't exist anymore. Then suddenly I would snap out of it, like a bad dream, and I was back among the living. I do not know, nor care, what brought me back from those metaphorical trips to a pitch-black basement. I was just glad when each episode was over. Over the years I had experienced and researched the symptoms of Depression enough to know that I had begun the lonely final trek down that dark road, again. It was like the movie Groundhog Day, or Deja Vu All Over Again, or Same Caca, Different Flies!

My moodiness increased and I became argumentative and downright combative at home. I was still an angry man. Any perceived slight or innocuous comment or action by anyone set me off. I yelled at the TV news. I yelled at other motorists when driving. I yelled at my dog. I argued with my wife. I drank too much. Then I started feeling so distraught that I would get a lump in my throat while watching a sad story or a commercial on TV.

Those thoughts of suicide came creeping back. I imagined crashing my truck into a tree or walking off a cliff or just eating a bullet. Then I would tell myself that any of those options was cowardly and would be too messy or put others in harm's way. I considered the old trick of running a hose from my truck's exhaust through an interior window of the cab until I just fell asleep. The list goes on. You would be surprised by how creative a person can be when looking for ways to kill themselves.

I put my wife through hell during these bouts of

darkness. She would cry and tell me sometimes she was afraid to come home from work and find me dead. She implored me to get help. I am not sure who or what it was that finally convinced me that I had to talk with a professional but, at long last, *I made the call.*

If you take anything away from my story, please take this one action, ASK FOR HELP. If I hadn't done so, I'm not sure I would have survived.

Chapter 14 -- My Road to Recovery

At last, I finally began to fully deal with my depression. My first therapist was a psychiatrist who prescribed a number of meds to address my Depression that included various antidepressants, mood stabilizers, and atypical antipsychotics. Unfortunately, before we could get into much discussion on my progress, he retired. Since the following therapists I saw were psychologists, that do not typically have drug prescription authority, I was forced to have my primary care physicians adjust my medications and prescribe new ones if the original ones were not working or produced unwanted side effects. Those doctors do not provide "talk therapy" like psychologists.

Consequently, I continued taking various meds while simultaneously being treated by several different psychologists, off and on, over the next few years. However, I wasn't seeing much progress, so I stopped seeing anyone for more than a year. It wasn't until I started seeing my current therapist, about three years ago, that I began to see real results in controlling my Depression.

My therapist has taught me to use a number of Cognitive, Behavioral, Acceptance and Interpersonal tools that have helped. These tools include keeping journals of negative thoughts that help me recognize Depression triggers; learning to receive positive pleasure from the little things in life;

meditation and breathing techniques to help me reduce depressive thoughts; learning to listen more and improve communication with people, including loved ones.

It took a while to find a mental health professional in the area that was taking new patients and who accepted my insurance. Very simply put, a therapist is a broad term that includes Psychiatrists, medical doctors who can diagnose and treat mental health conditions from a medical perspective and prescribe drugs. Psychologists, who hold a doctorate in psychology and provide mental healthcare that can include coping and emotional healing strategies; and Counselors, who are licensed to provide various types of mental wellness therapies along with counseling. Psychologists, with some exceptions, and Counselors do not prescribe medications. Even if your insurance does not cover mental health, try to find the funding somewhere. You will never make a better investment.

I would encourage you to choose any of these professionals. Most of those early antidepressant medications did make a difference, some did not. I was told that I could expect to try different meds and combinations until I found the right mix that helped the most.

Over the next few years, I saw four different therapists and continued to try various medications. Some of the antidepressants would work for a while until they didn't. I would then try other meds prescribed by my primary care doctor. Most people will likely react differently to the various meds so you just keep trying until you find the ones that help the most. I now regularly take two medications that work for me.

Although I was doing pretty well keeping The Bastard locked away, occasionally the dark feelings would start to well up again. Fortunately, using various tools the therapists had taught me, I managed to keep a lid on the Depression. I felt comfortable enough to stop seeing my last therapist. That lasted about two years until I started to have significant anxiety and mood swings again. This time I did not wait, I restarted visits to my psychologist. I explained to her what was happening again and that I needed a “refresher” course on previous things I had learned from her that were successful in tamping down my Depression.

Admittedly, I had let slide most of the self-care habits she taught me. For example, controlled breathing techniques; how to release thoughts and calm myself; to be grateful for the big and little things around me; to step back and avoid acting and speaking out of anger; to listen more and talk less; and to receive and accept the things that make me sad and then release them. One such action she taught me was to simply fling a stick into the Rio Grande during my daily walks along the bosque and imagine that the stick represented whatever was bothering me that day. As it floats away, I say goodbye to those feelings and watch them drift away, allowing those negative thoughts to leave my brain. If I had saved all those sticks, I could have a huge bonfire. My point here is to show you that there are lots of ways to make yourself feel better and keep The Death Monkey off your back.

But sometimes I forget these tools, or I find myself slacking off for a while and before I know it, the Big D starts slithering back in. That is what happened to me and why I went back to my therapist for help. Sometimes these methods do not always instantly make things better, but I just keep reminding myself that they *do* help if I keep working at it. Occasionally, I find myself beginning to spiral down again until I remember that these various mental exercises represent a life preserver for me. All I have to do is reach for it.

I would venture to say that most good therapists, besides just listening and being nonjudgmental, can teach you about these and other brain training methods that can help you deal with your Depression. Therapists are trained to help you draw out and discuss your innermost thoughts and troubles that consistently dump you into that well of despair. The goal is to give you the tools you need to climb out of that well. It is not easy, sometimes it is a daily struggle that you must work on, maybe with the help of medications.

Without sounding like your know-it-all cousin or some self-help guru on TikTok, I will say that you have to *want* to get better. Afterall, who the hell wants be sad, angry, apathetic, or suicidal? And I do not want to sound like a broken record (do you suppose anyone under 30 even knows what a vinyl record is? Maybe that's the 'radio guy' talking) but you need to know and believe that there is help out there. I will not preach to you about secular salvation, all I can do is tell my story in hopes that someone will see themselves in it and do what is right for them.

Late last year, I knew the current therapy was working for me as I watched my best friend Larry slowly slip away into dementia and physical deterioration which eventually led to his death. I felt better equipped mentally to deal with what was happening to him during his final days. After he died, using the tools given to me by my therapist, I managed to avoid the deep well of Depression I had experienced so many times in the past. Larry's passing still hurts, but I have learned how to process the pain by choosing to remember his face, his laughter, his kindness, and our brother-like connection over almost 70 years.

My doctor provided me with a number of other crisis

survival skills. I've learned not to act impulsively to a negative emotion, i.e., two shots of whiskey to take the edge off my anger over something a politician said or did. Instead of feeling overwhelmed with the day's to-do-list, I can simply splash cold water on my face and take a short break while breathing deeply. If I feel anxious, I can do something that makes me feel good, like walking along the river or just snuggling and petting my dog. These are just a small fraction of the many self-help tools my therapist has passed along. Even though I need to actively practice these things, I know they work to help keep that Depression Monkey off my back.

Chapter 15 -- Death Monkey Off Your Back!

Coming back to the beginning of this writing, my purpose was twofold:

1. -- Most importantly, to use my platform as a former popular radio personality to discuss suicidal thoughts caused by Depression and to show that even the seemingly happy-jokester had a very different side after the mics were off. This radio character known as 'The Bean' was and still is, like many people-maybe you, who have a difficult time dealing with daily sadness, hopelessness, and other adjectives commonly used to describe feelings linked to Depression. It really is like having a Death Monkey on your back but, you do *not* have to let it hitch a ride until it kills you. I want you to know that your Depression is not a sign of weakness or something to be ashamed about. You are not alone. It's okay to admit you need help and it is absolutely vital that you get that help.

2.-- Part of my reason for writing this is ego driven. I worked hard to achieve the things I did in my career as a broadcaster and I guess I just wanted people to know that besides portraying 'The Bean' on Albuquerque radio, I had a previous career as a serious and accomplished broadcast journalist. And after the 'goofy guy on the radio' stint, I was lucky enough to work in politics and then serve in state and county government.

It has taken years for me to open up to anyone other than therapists, my wife, and a few close friends and then to finally write down my story and how it has been affected by Depression. There are many people and events that I did not include here. In retrospect, the people are probably glad and some of the events would best serve as inspiration if I ever get around to writing fiction.

Again, it is my fervent hope that anyone who reads this can glean something helpful and can be applied in their own lives. And please understand that *anyone* can be suffering from Depression while no one around them is aware of it. Try to extend some grace if you do know what they are facing and just be a friend.

The producer in my head is giving me the wind it up signal. I want to thank all the people along the way that affected my life, good and bad, because all of it informed my existence as it stands today. I am especially grateful for those of you, who for years, daily let me into your lives through your radios. Be well and thanks for listening and reading.

And finally, as that guy known as 'The Bean' said when closing every show, Bueno Bye!

OVER AND OUT

Phil Sisneros

Acknowledgements

The Death Monkey Rides took a lifetime of experiences and more than a few years of fragmented notes, encouragement from friends, false starts and fear of sharing very personal aspects of my life to finally produce this project.

Most importantly I want to thank my wife, Debbie Sisneros, who helped me through the darkest days and who is still my role model for being happy.

My sincerest thanks also to Dr. Sarah Steele, Psy.D. and a few therapists before her for helping me discover, discuss and deal with my own Depression. My great appreciation and thanks to mental health professionals Paul D. Garver and Bryan Norman for reviewing and offering very helpful suggestions for this book. Author Carmen Alexander for reviewing and providing guidance. My friend Zack Freeman, who consistently encouraged me to keep trying to tell my story. Jose Antonio Ponce, of Jason's Music Publishing, for his excellent work in polishing and producing this book. Other friends and family who tolerated me over the years, not knowing how severe my Depression was. And last, but not least--thanks to The Death Monkey who rode my back, tried to kill me, and who finally caused me to seek help before he could accomplish that.

Acknowledgments

For the first time, thoughts of suicide floated in and out of my mind. I think my mind imploded, yet I confided in no one and managed daily to put on the happy face and demeanor of The Bean.~

The Death Monkey Rides

Having a "monkey on my back" is an idiom that can describe a burden, a heavy weight to carry, or a problem that won't go away. For me that monkey represented thoughts of suicide that became heavier and more frequent over time. I learned that my own mental Depression is what provided fertile ground for the monkey to grow. This animal clung to my back for years whispering in my ear that all my troubles would go away if I just worked up the courage to kill myself. Sometimes I agreed with the monkey of death.

Starting during childhood, that little bastard hitched a ride on my shoulders and got bigger and heavier as I grew up. He's still barely clinging to my back and still tries to talk to me occasionally. But with a lot of help from therapists and anti-depression medications, the monkey has become almost weightless, and I don't hear his voice anymore. With any luck he'll eventually be gone for good.

With professional treatment most people can learn how to deal with their Depression. I believe this illness can affect anyone, no matter who they are, what they do for a living or what face they wear in public. There is help out there and you deserve it.

Jason’s Music Publishing is a place where new and emerging authors, songwriters, musicians and film makers can come to produce their work without breaking their budget.

Jason’s Music Publishing does not ask to share copyright, publishing rights or revenue. For more information, go to http://jasonsmusicpublishing.com or reach out to us at contactjasonsmusic@gmail.com